*Rudy Wiebe
and His Works*

Rudy Wiebe (1934–)

SUSAN WHALEY

Biography

RUDY WIEBE: novelist, short-story writer, playwright, anthology editor, professor of creative writing, and Canadian historian and myth maker. A remarkable diversity has informed the thirty-year literary career of this Western writer, and it appears, with the recent publication of *My Lovely Enemy*, that Wiebe's vigour has not yet abated.

Rudy Henry Wiebe was born on 4 October 1934 in Fairholme, Saskatchewan, the second child of Abram J. and Tena (née Knelson) Wiebe. Rudy Wiebe's first childhood visions were shaped by the surrounding bush and prairie, and his imagination was fired by his parents' stories "of Russia, of czars and villages and Bolsheviks and starvation and anarchists and war and religious fights: all very good in their way because they kept the childish story-necessity alive . . . ."[1] As Mennonites, the elder Wiebes had been subjected to religious persecution in Russia and had fled to Canada in 1930, only a few years before Wiebe's birth. The Wiebe family spoke a Friesian dialect of Low German at home, and they were concerned with preserving the religious precepts for which they had been obliged to leave Russia. They were pioneers in the tiny community of Speedwell-Jackpine, Saskatchewan, which remained the family home for the first thirteen years of Rudy Wiebe's life. Wiebe remembers the harsh climate and difficult working conditions to which his family was subjected, and, even now, he vividly recalls the three long miles he had to trek to a one-room schoolhouse. "Towns and cities," says Wiebe, "with their paved streets, department stores, motor vehicles, electric lights and spacious bedrooms . . . inhabited the segment of my imagination reserved for Grimm's fairy tales and the Greek myths," and Canada itself seemed "a miracle" by virtue of the fact that "we could work and we had something to eat . . . ."[2] Initially, it was the emptiness and loneliness of his environment that impressed

Wiebe; together with his historical sense of the land, these early impressions continue as the main catalysts for his writing.

The Wiebe family moved to Coaldale, Alberta, in 1947, and Rudy began studies at the Alberta Mennonite High School. He entered the University of Alberta in Edmonton in 1953 as a first-year medical student but switched to the study of English literature during his second year. Encouraged in his writing by F. M. Salter, who had also been W. O. Mitchell's mentor, Wiebe won first prize in the National Federation of Canadian University Students' short-story contest, for "Scrapbook,"[1] when he was twenty-one years old. Wiebe graduated in 1956 with a Bachelor of Arts, and, in the same year, his short story "The Power" was chosen by Earle Birney to appear in *New Voices: Canadian University Writing of 1956*. During the year following his graduation, Wiebe worked as a research writer for the Glenbow Foundation in Calgary, Alberta. Then, presented with a Rotary International Fellowship for 1957–58, he spent the year studying at the University of Tübingen in West Germany. This prestigious award was followed by his being named an International Nickel Graduate Fellow (1958–59) and a Queen Elizabeth Graduate Fellow (1959–60). After his return to Canada from abroad, Wiebe married Tena F. Isaak, in March 1958, and recommenced studies at the University of Alberta, from which he received his Master of Arts in 1960. That same year, he also served in Ottawa as a foreign-service officer for the Government of Canada. In 1961 he completed theological studies at the Mennonite Brethren Bible College in Winnipeg, to earn his Bachelor of Theology, and began his career as an English teacher in a high school in Selkirk, Manitoba. He combined this vocation with further studies at the University of Manitoba during 1961 and worked as editor of *The Mennonite Brethren Herald* in Winnipeg from 1962 to 1963.

His first novel, *Peace Shall Destroy Many*, originated as his Master's thesis and was published in 1962. The novel presents a bleak look at a Mennonite community in Saskatchewan, and its publication raised no small amount of controversy in Canadian and American Mennonite circles. As a result, Wiebe resigned his position as editor of the Mennonite paper. He eventually left Manitoba to teach at Goshen College, Indiana, as assistant professor of English, from 1963 to 1967. In 1964 he studied creative writing at the University of Iowa and received a Canada Council bursary. With 1966 came the publication of his second novel, *First and Vital Candle*, a tale of the

Canadian North, which was adapted for radio in 1967. The following year, Wiebe and his family returned to Alberta; since then, Wiebe has taught at the University of Alberta in Edmonton, where he has been a full professor of creative writing since 1976. From 1978 to 1979, he was writer-in-residence at the University of Calgary.

With the publication of *The Blue Mountains of China* in 1970, it was quite evident that Wiebe's writing had taken a new and mature direction. His next novel, *The Temptations of Big Bear* (1973), brought him the coveted Governor General's Award for fiction. This book, which meticulously delineates the conflict between the Indians and the white man, and the final demise of native freedom, had taken him six years to research and write. His next novel, *The Scorched-Wood People* (1977), is a testament to the vision of Louis Riel and the Métis people.

Aside from his novels, Wiebe has produced a number of short stories and edited many short-story anthologies, which include: *The Story-Makers: A Selection of Modern Short Stories* (1970), *Stories from Western Canada* (1972), *Stories from Pacific and Arctic Canada* (1974, with Andreas Schroeder), *Double Vision: An Anthology of Twentieth-Century Stories in English* (1976), *Getting Here* (1977), *More Stories from Western Canada* (1980, with Aritha van Herk), and *West of Fiction* (1983, with Leah Flater and Aritha van Herk). The first collection of his own short stories, *Where Is the Voice Coming From?*, was published in 1974, and his first play, written in conjunction with Theatre Passe Muraille and entitled *Far as the Eye Can See*, was published in 1977. Wiebe has also written the script for a film version of his novel *The Mad Trapper* (1980), entitled *Death Hunt*. His most recent works are the collection of short stories entitled *The Angel of the Tar Sands and Other Stories* (1982) and the novel *My Lovely Enemy* (1983).

A family man, a teacher, and still very much a writer, Wiebe continues to reside in Edmonton with his wife, Tena, and their three children: Adrienne, Michael, and Christopher. Wiebe thinks of himself as "someone who's trying to live what the original Anabaptists were about," which means being "a radical follower of the person of Jesus Christ."[4] The 320 acres of bush, swamp, and rock that Wiebe owns, fifty miles southwest of Edmonton, attest to his devotion to the land and his intense awareness of it as both living presence and historical force. The majority of his fiction arises from his long-cultivated interest in native peoples, while the thematic bent and lyrical rhythm of much of his best work reveal Wiebe's religiousness and his natural musical inclination. Wiebe is highly conscious of his responsibility as an artist, and it is his integrity as a writer which most clearly defines him.

Tradition and Milieu

Rudy Wiebe's art is neither Christian, nor ethnic, nor regional, although each of these concerns certainly informs his work. Though he has been called "the only overtly Christian novelist among this country's important contemporary writers,"[5] Wiebe is the first to deny the presence of any overt propagandizing in his work: "I never consciously think of writing a so-called Christian novel . . . . I think of getting at, of building, a story; but I don't consciously say to myself, It's got to be a Christian story . . . . If you are what you are, and what you're making is any good, it's there anyway; you don't have to spell it out."[6] It is often suggested that as a member of an ethnic minority Wiebe is more naturally drawn to write sympathetically about other groups of outsiders, as his first five novels certainly demonstrate, but a glance at the stylistic diversity of the body of his work would surely discourage any attempt to classify Wiebe as merely a spokesman for minority cultures. Throughout his career, Wiebe has experimented with narrative technique, with stylistic devices such as stream of consciousness, and with various genres like drama, the short story, and the novel. Wiebe distrusts labels and so denies that he is only a regional writer, but he is eager to define his position in terms that demand reevaluation of critical attitudes towards such writers as himself. "One of the problems with regionalism," Wiebe contends, "is that everybody grabs for and writes about the same kinds of experiences. This results in a hackneyed school . . . . We haven't really had writers [in the West] who in their concentration on the particular have been able to subsume that and make it universal."[7] Western writers, according to Wiebe, have been preoccupied with the depression era, and the predominance of work concerning this one aspect of history "makes the West seem static and monotonous." Wiebe maintains that this is a false impression. "Things are not monotonous on the prairies. The plains just force you to look more closely at things to see change" (Melnyk, pp. 204–05).

"There is an authentic kind of western Canadian experience and I look upon myself as a prairie writer" (Melnyk, p. 208), Wiebe affirms, and in so doing, he implicitly aligns himself with such predecessors as Frederick Philip Grove, Sinclair Ross, and W. O. Mitchell. Where he most significantly differs from these writers is his sense — and in this Wiebe is not unlike Robert Kroetsch — that it remains impossible for a Canadian artist to create a tradition. Wiebe insists that whatever tradition we can claim is indigenous to the land: "What we have to do is dig up the whole tradition, not just the white one. It's not a recorded tradition, it's a verbal one" (Melnyk, p. 206). Wiebe emphasizes that the land *is* his tradition. He meticulously explores this world he knows; what he sees — the "infinite variety" of the prairies (Melnyk, p. 205) — is what inspires his work about the land. Canada need not seek for itself in the prefabricated myths of the numerous cultures of which it is comprised; its richest possible heritage has always existed in the land, and Rudy Wiebe serves as its main excavator.

Wiebe has voiced his admiration for Frederick Philip Grove, who, before leaving Europe to journey west to North America, was endowed, like Wiebe, with a much older, more established heritage. In his article "A Novelist's Personal Notes on Frederick Philip Grove," Wiebe outlines the influence Grove exerted on him as the first Canadian writer he had ever read. Before this illuminating experience, he had been primarily interested in European literature: in particular, "Victor Hugo captivated me . . . with his incredible hero Jean Valjean and the sewers of Paris" ("A Novelist's," p. 215). But Wiebe has since defined his own literary theory according to the finer points of Grove's work: Grove "was a writer who wrote mythically and imagistically about the world I knew. This cultivated European looked hard at my bush Canada, saw it, and found it not simply restrictive and hampering: it was merely different . . . . It is the person who looks at a particular world that counts . . ." ("A Novelist's," p. 216). This and Grove's belief that the ordinary man should have his story told are what essentially attract Wiebe. What Grove accomplished, and what Wiebe has adopted from him, is that method of transmuting immediate details from the self into story. Wiebe theorizes:

Fiction is always truer than fact in this sense; it is never possible to know all the facts about anything, even the very smallest act.

5

> The things done vanish with their doing; they can live only in a
> living memory, and the true story-teller has the unstoppable
> longing to capture these acts forever beyond memory. ("A
> Novelist's," p. 217)

But in his accolade to Grove, Wiebe rejects those attempts which
have been made to label Grove a realist; Wiebe redefines him as
something of a symbolist, and the reasons he delineates to support
this reveal his own aversion to being considered merely a realist
writer.

Wiebe identifies wisdom as the quality which pervades Grove's
work and which imbues it with "a high seriousness of *Weltan-
schauung*" ("A Novelist's," p. 223). This old-fashioned characteristic distinguishes Grove's fiction and leads Wiebe to utter a comment
that places himself and his artistic ideals counter to the prevailing
current: since New Criticism and exegesis are in, he claims, the
writer "has become a mechanical functionary who weaves a bit of
this here, adds a dash of that there, but the largest design of all, wisdom, is quite beyond him. It is not even expected" ("A Novelist's,"
p. 223). Wiebe's fidelity to the spirit of Grove's creativity brings
Wiebe into alignment with Western writers such as Sinclair Ross and
W. O. Mitchell, while his sense of community and his tendency
towards biblical hermeneutic, as critic David L. Jeffrey suggests,
draw him into Margaret Laurence's territory.[8] Wiebe has criticized
contemporaries Robert Kroetsch and Mordecai Richler for the limited dimensions of their protagonists, whose concerns are only personal — "I get a little impatient with the pipsqueaks who people
present-day fiction" ("A Novelist's," p. 220). Still, there remain certain thematic similarities between his own work about racial and religious minorities and that of artists such as Richler and Adele
Wiseman.

It is morally impossible for Wiebe to neglect a heritage which, he
insists, does not need creating but rather articulating. The vastness
of the prairie demands expression:

> . . . to touch this land with words requires an architectural
> structure; to break into the space of the reader's mind with the
> space of this western landscape and the people in it you must
> build a structure of fiction like an engineer builds a bridge. . . .
> You must lay great black steel lines of fiction, break up that

space with huge design and, like the fiction of the Russian steppes, build giant artifact.[9]

Wiebe is convinced that fiction is the most appropriate literary mode of the prairies, just as Tolstoy made it the mode of the Russian steppes. Long an admirer of Tolstoy, Wiebe considers him to have influenced the direction of his own writing. Far more than the simple necessity to recognize and define the self in terms of the surrounding immensity, Wiebe sees stories about the past as "meaning and life to us as *people*, as a *particular* people."[10] History is neither external nor peripheral to Canadians; and in Western Canada, says Wiebe, history "is no vacuum . . . but rather the great ocean of our ignorance as horizonless as the prairies themselves" ("On the Trail," p. 137). Occupying this illimitable space are a myriad of details and tiny facts — the indelible imprints of earlier times, of former inhabitants — which Wiebe scrupulously devotes himself to discovering. But these particles of the past to which the writer binds himself can both inhibit and illuminate his work. Wiebe describes the act of working from factual data as similar to "finding a bone, a petrified bone down by the creek and then finding the rest of it, and then . . . [piecing] together the pieces that make the dinosaur."[11] But the completed whole is, Wiebe recognizes, an illusion of life; it is a tenet of his artistic faith that the shaping of facts and events into story is important only insofar as it shows "the human meanings behind them."[12]

The search for "human meanings" is tied to Wiebe's didactic, heavily moralistic theory of art. Indeed, his assertion that art's purpose is "to make us better"[13] appears anachronistic. According to Wiebe, the impulse behind art is born from "the appreciation of what's beautiful, and what is evocative, and what is stimulating to you in your finest perceptions . . . . [G]reat art broadens you . . . ."[14] A story, as opposed to an actual demonstration, "is the perfect vehicle" for teaching moral qualities, which are always "concerned with ideals purer in the mind than in the actuality" (*SM*, p. xviii). But fears of whatever stern, dry style such gravity would seem to portend are quickly dispelled by some of Wiebe's more outstanding works such as "Did Jesus Ever Laugh?," *The Blue Mountains of China*, *The Temptations of Big Bear*, and *The Scorched-Wood People*.

Wiebe's moral stance informs his choice of subject matter. He has consistently attempted to transform what was formerly an oral tradition into a written one. In so doing, the myths enshrouding historical figures such as Big Bear and Louis Riel are peeled away and a new, more palpable reality is born. But Wiebe does not suggest that this reality is the product of impartial observation. In *The Temptations of Big Bear*, for example, his views are admittedly slanted in favour of the Indians. He sees much in common between Big Bear and certain biblical prophets, for they share "the sense of a heritage that has been sold out, that through ignorance or neglect has simply been left: and the voice very clearly says that you cannot neglect your inheritance like this . . . ."[15] Wiebe has consciously taken it upon himself to give minorities such as Indians, Métis, Eskimos, and Mennonites a voice.

If, as Wiebe believes, the past twenty years of Canadian fiction have gone a long way towards destroying "the myth that Canada is a classless, non-racist society,"[16] then a new tradition in Canadian letters has been launched, and Wiebe is certainly to be counted a prime instigator of it. In making native groups the centre of much of his fiction, Wiebe has brought sharply into focus the realities of Indian, Métis, and Eskimo life. Destroying a stereotype is not easy, but Wiebe has persevered and prevailed against that notion of the Indian "as a sometimes exotic but mostly deprived and drunken frill at the edges of our humor and realism."[17] His admiration for the innate poetic qualities in these people is quite evident, and especially so for the North dwellers who "have not yet told their stories. They have lived them, and sung them in poetry, but they have not told them in a way we explorers understand at our very core."[18] Now that the Canadian West has been more or less mapped, Wiebe predicts that the true direction for fiction is, inevitably, due north. Wiebe shares with the Eskimo their "absolute faith in the power of the word"[19] and admires them in their continuous battle with the elements. Certainly this same icy terrain plays a vital role in Wiebe's 1980 novel *The Mad Trapper*: the frozen landscape acquires a life of its own as witness to the ruthless chase of Albert Johnson by the Mounties. Here a blasted, isolate North symbolizes the lonely, detached state of the anonymous trapper's mind. The articulation of this last frontier — the North — thus remains of the utmost importance to Wiebe.

Critical Overview and Context

Canada's response to its own literature has always been somewhat provincial. At no time is this more apparent than when reviewing the body of criticism on Rudy Wiebe's fiction. Wiebe's rather eccentric adherence to religious themes and imagery has evidently prejudiced numerous critics against much of his earlier fiction. As a result, the fine stylistic experimentation in Wiebe's work has been virtually neglected. The increased complexity of both *The Temptations of Big Bear* and *The Scorched-Wood People* demanded greater critical attention to Wiebe's writing than their predecessors had called for, yet the appearance of these two books did not turn the critical tide in Wiebe's favour; indeed, the latter novel raised barely a scholarly peep. Despite the marked improvement in Wiebe's later novels, criticism of his fiction — with the exception of the insights of a few critics such as Allan Dueck, Ina Ferris, W. J. Keith, and Patricia Morley — has remained stagnant.

One of the first reviews following the publication of *Peace Shall Destroy Many* in 1962 heralded Wiebe as "a man who could well become one of Canada's major novelists."[20] Not all the reviews, however, were quite so positive. Wiebe's use of dialogue was justifiably criticized as too artificial and preachy in nature, and some critics found certain characters, such as Razia, "not entirely convincing."[21] Other reviewers at this time lamented the exaggeration and the tendency towards melodrama, yet praised the novel on the whole as "a moving work on a profound theme."[22] Mennonite reviewers, with the exception of Elmer F. Suderman, were moved as well — but to scorn. Suderman evaluated the book in aesthetic terms,[23] while the majority of Mennonite reviewers assumed a defensive posture and were thus unable to approach the novel on its own terms. Decidedly odd is the fact that the novel dropped from critical sight completely after 1963 and only received renewed attention during the early years of the following decade. Of the more recent commentators, William H. New applauded what remains one of Wiebe's outstanding qualities as a writer, "his careful way with words,"[24] while Frank Davey persisted in labeling Wiebe an "overtly Christian advocate."[25] It took Patricia Morley's 1977 study of the comic elements in Wiebe, *The Comedians: Hugh Hood and Rudy Wiebe*, to rekindle interest in the structural aspects of the novel. Hers remains one of the most astute, innovative looks at

Peace Shall Destroy Many, simply because she took so little in the novel for granted.

The reviews of *First and Vital Candle* were not much more positive than those which greeted *Peace Shall Destroy Many*. J. M. Stedmond, for example, felt that "some of the writing has a certain crude power, but there is a good deal of sloppiness in both form and content, including lapses into an incoherent version of stream-of-consciousness based apparently on Gerard Manley Hopkins' sprung rhythms . . . ."[26] B. Pomer bewailed "Wiebe's hummocky prose style,"[27] and most other reviewers of the novel criticized its characterization. Those most sympathetic to Wiebe's work excused his characters in favour of the novel's message, but the more balanced reviews found fault with both aspects of the book. It was too didactic, and its characters fanatic and unconvincing.

In his third novel, *The Blue Mountains of China*, Wiebe reverted to his earlier consideration of Mennonite conflicts. As a result, this book is frequently critically evaluated together with *Peace Shall Destroy Many*. *The Blue Mountains of China* attracted more attention than the earlier two novels combined and seems to have been quite favourably received. It was seen as "a story that embodies religious faith instead of stating it,"[28] and, further yet, as "an epic history."[29] It was also the first of his novels to be linked with other major Canadian works, such as Frederick Philip Grove's *Our Daily Bread*[30] and A. M. Klein's *The Second Scroll*.[31]

The Temptations of Big Bear triggered in some reviewers their dormant sense of shared guilt for the sins of their land-hungry forefathers. An example of this kind of critical attitude can be found in Allan Bevan's Introduction to the New Canadian Library edition of the novel.[32] Allen Dueck, in his assessment of the novel, suggested that ". . . one of Wiebe's central concerns . . . is to repudiate the biased white view of this history and to rectify its errors";[33] of the dozens of reviews that appeared, few ventured to comment beyond this historical, referential level. And critics have not yet agreed on the merit of what is obviously the novel's strength — that is, the complexity and fluidity of the narrative.[34] At least most critics felt on slightly more familiar — "more purely Canadian"[35] — ground in discussing the work, although they generally experienced those same pangs of discomfort at what seemed to be further evidence of Wiebe's religiosity. Critics obsessed with the lack of a Canadian mythology were pleased to claim the book as satisfying the national need for one, and *The Temptations of Big Bear* was described in terms ranging from epic to elegy. [36]

With the 1977 appearance of *The Scorched-Wood People*, it became apparent that certain critical opinions on Wiebe's work would persist. The amount of attention paid the novel has been modest and, as formerly, quite diverse in viewpoint. Ken Adachi felt it superior to the run-of-the-mill historical novel, yet found the novel's design "enormous and somewhat over-detailed, even tedious . . . ; [Wiebe's] characters often inscrutable."[37] Marian Engel was very enthusiastic about "this awesome novel,"[38] while a Western reviewer described *The Scorched-Wood People* as "not the least turgid book [he had] ever read."[39] Even George Woodcock could not work up much sympathy for a subject so obviously dear to him: "Unfortunately Rudy Wiebe has been unable . . . to separate the purpose of historical fiction, which is to give us a plausible image and feeling of the past, from that of the historical moralist, which is to apportion blame, signal merit and formulate lessons."[40] On the other hand, W. J. Keith was prompted to see in Wiebe's storytelling propensity similarities to the art of Sir Walter Scott and Leo Tolstoy.[41] R. P. Bilan lauded *The Scorched-Wood People* as a more successful novel than *The Temptations of Big Bear*,[42] and Sam Solecki was impressed by Wiebe's translation of history "into eschatology."[43]

The Mad Trapper (1980) received negative reviews, and no small amount of furor was raised about the authenticity of the historical statements in that novel.[44] What is perhaps most disturbing about the reception of each of Wiebe's novels remains simply that critics, whether in appreciation or dissent, have discussed his work in superficial and general terms.

Nineteen eighty-one saw the publication of two critical evaluations of Rudy Wiebe's fiction. The first, *A Voice in the Land: Essays by and about Rudy Wiebe*, edited by W. J. Keith, is divided into six sections: each includes previously published articles by Wiebe and by scholars of his work, and, taken in order, they outline the progress of his career in terms of his major novels, up to and including *The Scorched-Wood People*. The essays chosen for the volume are solid, insightful ones, but of particular note are the four interviews with Wiebe. Finally, the bibliography is highly selective and includes secondary sources from 1973 on.

The second work, W. J. Keith's *Epic Fiction: The Art of Rudy*

Wiebe, is a fairly thematic and biographical approach to Wiebe and his work. Keith does not account for much other scholarship on Wiebe, but he does include a useful bibliography in this general critical introduction to Wiebe's novels. The discussion ranges from *Peace Shall Destroy Many* to *The Scorched-Wood People*; Keith devotes a chapter to each work and rather uncritically explores Wiebe's transformation into a major Canadian writer. Wiebe's work still awaits a more balanced, penetrating analysis.

My Lovely Enemy (1983) occasioned the usual mixed reviews. Some critics, like Marty Gervais, were downright scornful,[45] while other readers, like Alan Dawe, were awestruck without quite knowing why.[46] Most reviewers seemed plainly baffled by this new direction in Wiebe's work.

As I hope to show, Wiebe's continual exploration and reiteration of Prairie and Northern history in stylistically innovative ways is anything but the self-indulgent exercise most critics have been content to see in his novels.

Wiebe's Works

Wiebe's first novel, *Peace Shall Destroy Many*, is set in the northern wilds of Saskatchewan during 1944. The war is still very much a fact, but it remains *out there*; in Wapiti, life goes undisturbed. The plot centres on the lives of Mennonite settlers who have deliberately sought an isolated environment in order to preserve their Christian ideals. Wapiti physically locks its inhabitants into their devotion and blocks out the threatening external world in accordance with the rigorous demands of Peter Block, the community's leader. Thom Wiens's unquestioning faith and allegiance to those standards set by Block are subjected, during the seasons of one year, to numerous assaults. Inevitably, Wiens is seized by doubts, many of which concern his people's practice of nonparticipation in the war effort. The drone of planes passing overhead serves as a reminder that the wartorn world exists despite Wapiti's self-righteous pacifism, and it provides a constant backdrop to the conflicts inside the community. One after another, Mennonite ideals are revealed to be hollow. While professing the principle of peace towards one's neighbours, Block demonstrates his hypocrisy time and again by his animosity towards the Métis and Indians employed as workers in the community.

Point of view in this *Bildungsroman* approximates the objectivity of the camera's eye, which records events without ever commenting on what it observes, and which, in this case, is privy to the internal thoughts as well as the external actions of each character. This narrative perspective is consistent throughout the novel; its ostensible function is mimetic — that is, the narrative is always expressed in literal, or at least in referential, terms.

The narrative is divided into four parts. Each part coincides with a particular season of the year and is in turn further divided into four chapters.[47] The fourth season, which is winter, proves to be an exception to this structure — it includes one extra chapter. Each seasonal division is introduced by a short "Prelude" that presents a backdrop for the scene about to unfold. But Wiebe first establishes the thematic and symbolic fabric of his story in the Foreword, where he explains how the Mennonites came to exist and where he also signals his interest in them as "a religious nation without a country,"[48] a nation similar to the wandering Israelite tribes. This is followed by a further indication of Wiebe's didactic intent, an epigraph from Daniel viii.23–25: a proud, ambitious man is to be broken in the course of the narrative — a foreshadowing of the final, apocalyptic vision towards which tensions build.

But subsequent to this unsettling taste of things to come is the "Prelude" to spring; its innocent affirmation of beneficent nature and of youthful vigour undercuts completely what has just preceded it. The tenor of this lyrical tribute to spring is heavily symbolic; in the first paragraph, two references are made to "crossroads" (p. 9), and the importance of water imagery is also intimated. The first chapter in this section again diminishes the effect of the epigraph. The reader is introduced to Thom Wiens, who, still strong in the faith of his forefathers, works the land to the thunder of planes overhead. Silently he curses them until he recalls himself to his purpose:

> Pulling his feet up hard with each step, he sensed within himself the strength of his forefathers who had plowed and subdued the earth before him. He, like them, was working out God's promise that man would eat his bread in the sweat of his face, not pushing a button to watch a divine creation blaze to earth. (p. 12)

This literal adherence to the Bible is rendered ironic by the end of the first chapter; ". . . war prices had almost cleared them of their debt" (p. 22), Thom reflects, until the planes reappear and he curses them as before: "Godless heathen, he thought" (p. 22). The outside world constantly imposes itself on the hypocritical peace of the community; the drone of war planes provides an ironic chorus throughout the narrative, until, at the novel's end, the outlook on life that the planes represent assumes a greater viability. The final sentence of the last section, which concerns winter, ironically signals a renewal through the "guns [that] were already booming in a new day" (p. 239). The novel's structure, therefore, is dependent upon the cyclical connotations associated with the seasons; but the expectations aroused by certain individual seasons — spring and winter in particular — are inverted. The beginning of the novel, which occurs in spring, coincides with the end of Thom Wiens's complacent faith in his people's ideals, and the end of the action, which occurs in winter, anticipates his new awareness.

The main focus of the novel rests upon the inhabitants of Wapiti. But Wiebe also provides a larger perspective, which heightens the already ironic incongruity between the community's ideals and its hypocritic reality. For that larger, vaguely threatening world surrounding the Mennonites is most profoundly felt in its absence. When Joseph Dueck, Thom's mentor, finally leaves Wapiti to join the Restricted Medical Corps, he is heard from again only as a ghost; his characterization dwindles until he is but a voice crying from the wilderness of war and depravity, calling the Mennonites to a new consciousness. Thus there is a constant telescoping of this outer, macrocosmic world into the isolated, microcosmic community of Wapiti, and Wiebe persistently reminds the reader of this double perspective. He has fabricated a Chinese-box-like narrative structure, successfully merging temporal and spatial dimensions into an integrated whole.

Wiebe's handling of time is superb. Time-in-the-story runs from spring to Christmas of the same year, forming an incomplete cycle. The plot unfolds in a strictly chronological manner, to the extent that divisions in the structure correspond directly to the narrative tenor. A steady rhythm envelops the reader as his or her sense of time comes to concur with that of the novel. Not only is the internal structure of *Peace Shall Destroy Many* circular, but, further, a circuit is established between reader and novel as time-in-the-story, or fictional time, overtakes objective, or real, time.

Even more disturbing to Thom than the impression of another world existing simultaneously beyond his own is that eerie sense of historical presence which arises in the summer section of the novel. A Mennonite named Herman has married Madeleine, the great-granddaughter of Big Bear and a recent convert to Christianity: "Hearing her tell of Big Bear, Louis Riel, Wandering Spirit, Thom glimpsed the vast past of Canada regarding which he was as ignorant as if it had never been: of people that had lived and acted as nobly as they knew and died without fear" (p. 111). That Mennonites are not the only people with a heritage dawns on Thom forcefully; the very Indians and Métis that the Mennonites abuse are descendants of tribes that used to roam the land freely. When Thom discovers a buffalo skull rotting in the field, a whole new dimension opens to him; he had never understood before that his own past was not also the land's: "White man reckoned places young or old as they had had time to re-mould them to their own satisfaction" (p. 82), he thinks. The piece of bone conjures up a variety of images in his mind, of the Indians that might have lain in wait for the beast, and of other scenes of "a whole world lost" (p. 83). And so, another temporal vista is revealed; the sense of time past, like the spatial sense of a world encompassing Wapiti, is a threatening one, for it forces the Mennonites out of their self-imposed segregation. Wiebe implies that they must come to comprehend themselves and their destiny as part of an ongoing cycle in time as well as in geographical location.

This insistence upon cycles, as upon certain symbols, is at times heavy-handed. During the winter section, for instance, Wiebe constantly reinforces the correspondence between the physical ebb and flow of nature and the spiritual movement of man in answer to it: ". . . the whole cycle of the seasons was an endless battle to retain existence" (p. 199). Wiebe's reliance upon fairly pedestrian natural and religious symbols is also regrettable. That well-worn symbol of the moth darting too near the flame is used in reference to Joseph Dueck, whose confrontations with the Mennonite elders leave him somewhat singed and necessitate his departure. Fortunately, Joseph leaves the scene early, and the reader is thereafter subjected to only small doses of his didacticism in his letters to Thom. But the absolutely rational moments of insight that punctuate Thom's coming to awareness do slow down the narrative. Witness, for example, this rendering of how Thom's conscience pricks him to acknowledge his own hypocrisy in refusing to visit Herman and his half-breed wife:

Thom's mind leaped to a justification: he had thought about revisiting Herman — several times, but there was never an opportunity at the moment of thought and — he caught himself, ashamed. He could judge others well enough. (p. 111)

Conversation is also marred by undue ponderousness. Even youngsters speak unnaturally, so that conversations like those between Thom and Annamarie, which anticipate a rising awareness of love for each other, remain flat and dull — mere conveniences for imparting information to the reader in order to further the plot:

> "Does the Restricted Medical Corps have to train like that too — with rifles and all?" Annamarie asked . . . .
>
> He said, picking [blueberries], "No. That's one of the odd things about their training. The restricted medicals never handle firearms of any kind. He [Joseph] writes they run around with stretchers and medical packs while the others carry rifles and shells."
>
> Margret rose to move farther. "Wow!" she yawned, "this is a good patch." (p. 92)

At this point, Wiebe shows little ear for the effective rendering of dialogue, but this is mostly attributable to the oppressive subject matter his characters continually expound.

There are, however, many redeeming passages of lyrical prose. As H. R. Percy notes, Wiebe "uses language with skill and courage."[49] Consider this description of Thom's perception of the land, in which the very rhythm of the prose complements what it describes:

> . . . he liked the earth as it unfolded itself like the roll of a filleted fish to a thin knife. Packed by the snows, it twisted free and lay open, crumbling at the edges, intruding no questions, offering itself and its power of life to the man who proved his belief with his calloused hand. And the believers went on turning its page, while round the world it was wounded to death by slashing heathen tank-tracks. (p. 18)

Here, the word, as spoken by God and translated in the Bible, is with the land. Man must work this earth in order to reap benefit from the sown word. God's word, though, is fruitful, whereas man's proves empty. "How can man's *words* ever change anything?" queries Thom (p. 62), for all he encounters in Wapiti is "the familiar, useless, circle of their talk" (p. 69), devoid of corresponding action. Thom's quest lies in coordinating his beliefs with meaningful action, just as the artist's ultimate goal lies in synchronizing content with form.

Some of his early short stories should be mentioned because they are so much of a piece with his early novels. "Scrapbook" (1956), "The Power" (1956), "Tudor King" (1964), and "Millstone for the Sun's Day" (1967) all deal with death. "Scrapbook," which brought Wiebe first prize in a short-story contest when he was twenty-one years old, depicts a boy's coming to terms with his invalid sister's death. "The Power" involves the deaths of two children in a fire while their parents have gone to buy them gifts. "Tudor King" describes two young brothers stumbling upon an old hermit and his dog dead inside his snowbound cabin. Finally, "Millstone for the Sun's Day" — thematically similar to Shirley Jackson's "The Lottery" — details a ritual sacrifice: a young boy is chosen to precipitate the death of his schoolteacher, who just happens to be this year's martyr. Most of the stories unfold in God-forsaken country; nature is always menacing and unkind, except, ironically, in "Millstone for the Sun's Day," where the sun shines benignly on all the barbaric proceedings below. There is always an archetypal family involved, and the deaths portrayed are all fairly grotesque. Wiebe seems to have been concerned more with cathartic effect than with innovative style; still, there is evidence in the stories of the language control that characterizes his later work. The scream which wakes young Buddy, in "Scrapbook," is virtually heard by the reader in this description of it:

> The screaming came again. It occupied his bent body completely, that inhuman scream, as if he and it were alone in a universe; it drowned his brain until he could not hear it for the sound, and then it fell horribly, as if stretched beyond elasticity
> . . . . [50]

First and Vital Candle is thematically akin to *Peace Shall Destroy Many*. It centres on a forty-year-old man named Abe Ross who returns to Winnipeg after twelve years in the arctic. He is alone, lonely, and fleeing a past that includes memories of a vindictive father, called Adam, and the father's self-righteous curses on the first-born son who has disobeyed him. That this is what really disturbs Abe is not revealed until the middle of the novel. Until that time, Abe is shown trying to assuage his loneliness in the streets of Winnipeg. The beautiful, solitary woman he follows home one night represents an ideal that as yet lies beyond his grasp. He later attends a cocktail party only to discover the emptiness, the barely stifled boredom, which the glittering guests attempt to disguise. All is unreal and undesirable to Abe until he is sent to Frozen Lake in northern Ontario. He assumes a one-year post as the Frobisher store manager there, and in his battle to understand and be known by the Ojibwa and to undermine the evil of his competitor, Sig Bjornesen, Abe comes to resolve his own inner turmoil. This is accomplished with the help of Josh and Rena Bishop and Sally Howell, who, as devout Christians, remain with the Indians in order to teach them. Sally, with whom Abe eventually falls in love, helps him to come to terms with the memories that unsettle him. But Abe is ultimately doomed to wrestle with his faith alone; Sally dies, and Abe carries on in solitude, troubled and unredeemed. Abe's quest for self is essentially the same as the one which faces Thom at the end of *Peace Shall Destroy Many*.

Wiebe employs symbolism even more deliberately here. The names, as in the first novel, are laden with biblical connotations. Even the geographic locale, Frozen Lake, "is an image of man without God."[52] Sig Bjornesen, with his demonic laugh and red face, proves to be the incarnation of evil; it is he who supplies the Indians with yeast for home-brew, and who instills them with fear and distrust. There also exists the eerie presence of the inexplicable; Wiebe makes the most of Sig's strange power over the natives and of resident shaman Kekekose's communing with spirits in order to save the dying man on whom Sig has placed a curse. Again, Wiebe relies a good deal on natural and religious imagery. All of the action unfolds in the wild, cruel beauty of the swamp-, rock-, and tree-dotted northland.

What is most remarkable about the novel is its design. Wiebe experiments in *First and Vital Candle* with narrative voice and structure, and the result is again antilinear. Cycle imagery is still important because it complements the novel's structure; sections of the novel are arranged according to seasons, and connotations evoked by particular seasons are inverted, as they are in the earlier novel. But Wiebe throws time-in-the-story out of joint in *First and Vital*

Candle; alternate parts of the story find Abe lost in a first-person narrative sequence about his past in the arctic, at school, in the army, and as a child at home. Parts ɪɪ, ɪᴠ, and ᴠɪ move backward in first-person narrative time, while the odd-numbered parts continue forward, narrating present story-time in the past tense from an objective, camera-eye view. This innovative structure allows Wiebe greater liberty in terms of style, and the result is an altogether engaging narrative.

Point of view, then, alternates, and this permits Wiebe to develop a narrative voice that recounts events in both past and present tense, from inside and outside Abe, and that instructs as it analyzes what has just occurred. Part ɪ of *First and Vital Candle* consists of three chapters, all narrated in a third-person, central-intelligence voice, which roams at will within and outside the personae it observes. The Kinconnell party, for instance, affords wonderful opportunities to expose all that is hollow in civilized, sophisticated life:

> The thunder of the beat in his ears and the clash-and-clasp shudder of their bodies were one now. Once when she hung back in his arms, only her body moving, her eyes hollows in the faded light reflected from outside and her open mouth a pink-rimmed hole, . . . he shuddered at the frightful decay of what he had once thought her loveliness. [53]

The only reality remains the music. The "St. John's Passion" that had so captivated Abe earlier in the evening is replaced by a demonic rhythm: ". . . the heavy off-beat of the bass was such as Bach had never written. It boomed like a giant viol of elemental humanity plucked at the very base where strings nub in flesh" (p. 38). These metaphors evoke quite a different vision than that in the earlier novel. Though Wiebe generally proves much better at describing rural scenes than city life, still, the rhythm of his language here captures something of urban inhumanity: "Immediately the crowds irked him, their ceaseless noisy lurching like walruses, advertising assaulting" (p. 43). Wiebe's control of language is more apparent in this second novel. The third-person narrative voice of Part ɪ occasionally modulates into stream of consciousness:

> Out of some corner of himself he heard with vision-like clarity that one male voice he had long given up hope of forcing into

oblivion reading from the Bible, morning and evening, and among all the thundered "thou-shalts" and "thou-shalt-nots" of damnation that forever ruled what even in this moment of past clairvoyance he knew completely without attempting to remember, there came this occasional call of recognized human break-down — a far away hesitant whisper of forgiveness? — he broke the thought and saw the mud turtle sunning on a spar beyond the shadow of the bridge. (pp. 44–45)

Here Abe's consciousness is interrupted by voices from the past. His father's is the voice that dominates; occasionally, though, Abe's older, forgiving self whispers, disrupting his store of resentment. This interplay of voices recurs throughout the novel; the pent-up bitterness and grief they evoke finally explode into the mainstream of Abe's consciousness:

the one last act of love and decency paid to her now so long dead recognized at last as nothing but the final twitch of excuse to scream back at his voice still pounding in my ear, cursing and forever disowning me and forbidding me the right to step on his land, to scream back at him every year again, "You slave driver! You God damn stingy slave driver! Working us all to death to buy your God damn stinking soul into heaven!" (p. 305)

Action is suspended; the breathless release is all. Such abandon inevitably occurs in the sections where Abe unfolds his own past in present time. The only exception is Part II, in which the story of Oolulik is recounted.

This particular section has been published separately as a short story.[54] It stands well on its own, for it is a captivating tale of the North. Within the novel, its presence is a highlight. Thematically, it serves as a backdrop for all that will face Abe in his dealings with Indians. The tragedy of Oolulik and her people is simply that their beliefs in the spirits who rule the natural world have been annihilated by the white man and replaced with words and rituals that even he does not believe in. The fact remains: as the white man invades their land, the deer leave and the Eskimo starve. What is stylistically intriguing, though, is the way Wiebe integrates snatches of song and prayer into the narrative flow:

Eyaya — eya
Where have gone the deer,
And the people of the deer?
Eyaya — eya.

(p. 82)

With this song of mourning, Oolulik banishes the formalized incantations of the white man's religion; the song, in its haunting simplicity, proves more memorable than the classical, formal Bach alluded to earlier and foreshadows the Indian chants and the personal prayers of the Bishops and Sally Howell.

Dialect, too, is effectively handled by Wiebe. For instance, Art Griffin's erratic mode of speech labels the man he is. Witness the lack of exchange between him and Abe as they meet for the first time:

> "Sonofagun it's about time! Put her there, man, I've waited a long time for somebody!" His hand in Abe's was as tense as a wire, "Every day waitin' for that damn plane. I've got everythin' stacked and ready to go — just throw a coupla things in the bag." (p. 108)

Wiebe also presents an interesting way of introducing a speaker's thoughts even while that character is speaking. For instance, Abe answers Sally concerning a particular Indian girl she was teaching and has not seen for a while:

> "I don't know, I was only over once" — You couldn't dream girlie what nerve I have to screw up to face the few in the store leave alone walk over and smile at them in front of their own houses as if no Tuesday night ever — "Sunday afternoon she was with some women, listening." (p. 313)

These undercurrents intensify the reader's understanding of Abe's psychological make-up.

The structure of *First and Vital Candle* is not quite as complex as that of *Peace Shall Destroy Many*. One year of Abe's life is accounted for, beginning in the late Winnipeg spring and finishing in the early northern spring. The narrative is divided into seven parts, just as a week has seven days. The even-numbered parts contain one chapter each, and the odd-numbered parts, from two to five chapters each.

Narrative stance in the even parts varies; "Oolulik," for instance, is a completely credible, first-person narrative, while Part IV is the work of an internal camera-eye, which gives way to a montagelike effect. With Part VI, the narrative reverts to the first-person stance. The odd-numbered sections, unlike the even, are arranged chronologically and are narrated in the past tense. But there is more than one past evoked in the tale; Wiebe's multiple perspectives force into the foreground, not only Abe's personal history, but also the cultural heritage of both the Ojibwa and the Eskimo. What is most significant is that the vista of the future is not considered until the end of the novel, when there is really no alternative. At Sally's grave, Abe is struck by the necessity of living on:

> He looked at the clods of earth, the cross, the pussy-willows and the little stakes; he understood that this spot would never again be of absolute importance to him because all that she had been and promised to be was flickering, alive in him. Though it made the life he still had to live hardly less fearful. (p. 354)

As in *Peace Shall Destroy Many*, the novel ends in apocalypse, and Abe, except for his memories of Sally and the promise she has represented, is alone as at the beginning. Fortunately, the devastation is more credible than in the earlier novel.

Wiebe's concerns remain the same in *First and Vital Candle* as they were in *Peace Shall Destroy Many*. The land, the "oppression, almost threat" (p. 221) of it, is inexpressible, which is why it remains a threat. Yet words are the real oppressors, as Josh explains to Abe: "It takes an educated man to be less human than a heathen . . . . Thinking he can logically explain everything that happens" (p. 145). His obsession with naming, with knowing, is precisely what impedes Abe's acceptance of the personal Christianity lived by the Bishops and Sally, as well as of the pagan spirituality of the Ojibwa. ". . . [W]ords themselves are what's impossible . . ." (p. 54), Abe knows, as is that preoccupation with intellectualizing even the most inexplicable of events.[55] The return of his two-months-lost revolver to him by Kekekose proves to Abe that ". . . he could not trust his eyes or the known fit of the gun in his hand or the faint mustiness . . . much less shape in his mind what had actually happened to him" (p. 157). Wiebe would seem to suggest that a more intuitive, or instinctive, response to life is needed; Sally tells Abe that she feels God speak to her (p. 321), but Abe cannot accept this until he opens himself, at the novel's end, to Sally's spiritual presence. The same didactic bent informs both of Wiebe's first two novels, and certain characters in the second resemble those in the first. Joseph Dueck, for example, is transformed into a combination of Josh Bishop and the old man Abe and Jim meet at a traffic light in Winnipeg. This latter character is quite expendable; luckily, however, Wiebe has crafted a more believable character in Josh than in Joseph. All in all, *First and Vital Candle* remains the more mature and innovative effort.

The years between the publication of *First and Vital Candle* and *The Blue Mountains of China* witnessed a marked maturation in Wiebe's narrative technique. A story entitled "Did Jesus Ever Laugh?" signals the pivotal point in this rich period of his career; it has been frequently anthologized since its first appearance in 1970, but has been all too quickly dismissed as simply "a chilling expression of fundamentalist fanaticism."[56] The narrative both grips and terrifies because Wiebe so meticulously reveals the depths of a psychotic mind. This vision is still apocalyptic, as in the earlier short fiction, but in this case the cataclysm is entirely warranted.

The story begins as an interior monologue in the present. The reader is immediately alerted to the icy deliberateness of the narrator; he is both scriptwriter and director of the little scenario about to unfold. The setting is a high-rise apartment building in Edmonton. Here the narrator feels assured of finding "one at least. You'd think so, wouldn't you, but you can't count on it; I've tried a few."[57] There is one female to be chosen for the ritual slaughter, it seems, although details unfold slowly in the narrator's own time. He is in no hurry; his sentences are short and matter-of-fact, but they barely hide the grim irony of his every thought: "They say Billy Graham could be coming next fall, but it's probably too much to pray for" (p. 57). It is "too much to pray for" only because such evangelical revivals usually prove excellent hunting-grounds for victims. Devoid of feeling and human contact, the narrator is "just eyes, waiting" (p. 58). While looking for his cue to enter the action, he is irritated by things in the setting he cannot alter, like the sun: "It's terrible; I stand there feeling my blood move, the warm air washing over my face. It's so bad then I even forget the words" (p. 58). Such reactions he cannot explain, though he is rational enough in his statement of them.

Once immersed in these distasteful associations, the narrator begins to ramble in what resembles stream-of-consciousness style:

. . . you wonder how many you maybe missed just like that
because you were hopeless even while you're sitting up, slowly,
careful, feeling it, letting it soak into you again as you're
looking and moving, always like the first time at that circus and
dead-white up high against the canvas the white leg starts out,
feeling slowly along something you can't see but it must be
there . . . , and then so sudden you haven't seen the move she's
standing complete, alone, . . . above everything on nothing.
Though you know there has to be a wire. (p. 58)

The drama is to unfold to music — his own version of "Leave the
dance with me sweet Sally" (p. 59) — and he is adamant that the
action must proceed neither more nor less quickly than he can sing
the verses of the ballad. Snatches of it recur throughout the narrative, recalling him to his duty. So too are bits of others' conversation
assimilated into his monologue, and these are rendered completely
banal to contrast more pointedly with his own poetic flow. Once he
spots his target, however, the narrative shifts to include, in quotation
marks, her responses to his presence. But there is never any real dialogue; his own answers are merely extensions of his earlier monologue. She remains a silhouette, the backdrop against which he will
assert himself:

. . . I'm hearing her, I guess, where she stands aside against the
coat closet in the grey apartment hall, talking, shifting as I
move so there's thirty inches between us, steady, as I reach for
the door . . . the light . . . from the window like bullets spraying
from her black solid lovely shape . . . . (p. 61)

Tension builds as he prompts both himself and the woman; she,
however, does not always respond properly to her cues. His running
commentary upon each of their moves is delivered in a positively
chilling fashion, especially when he describes his murder of the
mother-in-law:

An instant is enough; a grey bun of hair on the bed facing the
other way and a quilt over the shoulders . . . . There's hardly a
twitch and it's done in a flick . . . . (p. 64)

People are always seen obliquely and impersonally; as the action proceeds, he becomes increasingly enmeshed in his own psychotic turmoil, and the other players on this stage of his design become more obscure. Yet the narrator remains completely lucid about everything he does, even when the narrative slows down to admit this kernel of his discontent: "There is, of course, no reason in the world why a human being should laugh" (p. 65). God is dead, he moans, and with Him all sense of guilt. The narrative loosens as it unfolds, until, near the end of the story, it is almost complete stream of consciousness:

> Sheep   the range flat grey powdered rock dusted in hollows
> to grey chewed root sheep-like clouds, white on grey-green,
> white on the streaky blue   the horizon so far and straight
> the hills turning on a shimmer of griddle heat (p. 69)

Narrative and subject matter are tightly integrated — inseparable, in fact — and all the more horrific because the entire action occurs in the present. The outcome is as inevitable as the narrator, undistinguished except by his psychosis, is deliberate.

Wiebe's third novel, *The Blue Mountains of China*, is a richly designed tapestry, in which the threads mingle and interweave, concerning the lives of four Mennonite families that have had to leave Russia in search of religious tolerance. The Friesens, the Epps, the Reimers, and the Driedigers all relate the story of their exodus and of life in the new land; some go to Canada, others to Paraguay and Brazil. The novel consists of thirteen chapters, four of which revolve around the life of one character, yet each chapter is capable of standing entirely on its own. A different point of view informs each chapter, and within chapters even that particular narrative stance is often distorted. But despite the widely disparate experiences recounted, there exists a real unity of design and intention, which becomes more apparent with the reading of each successive chapter. Wiebe is more stylistically innovative in *The Blue Mountains of China* than in his two preceding novels, and it is a far more demanding work in terms of its structure. However, the same themes that link all of his work are still much in evidence; the search for meaning and the struggle to retain a shared past, a tradition, and a sense of family animate all of the personal tales that make up the novel.

While some characters reappear during the course of the novel, others do not. Nor are the intervals consistent at which they do return. Narrative perspective, tone, characterization, and setting all differ from chapter to chapter. Wiebe has created a deliberately disjointed narrative in which a reader is disoriented at every turn. As Ina Ferris aptly puts it, the novel "engages the reader in his own struggle in a narrative wilderness."[58] There really exists a sense of chaos in terms of narrative structure that is absolutely germane to the very diverse experiences and myriad images with which the reader is assailed. Whatever expectations one might harbour about the history of an ethnic group, they are quickly shattered, for history is not linear, according to Wiebe. Rather, it is as unpredictable as are its many disconnected parts; only considered in totality does the fabric's design reveal so much more than any one of its threads.

The first section introduces the one character who remains the novel's only claim to consistency. "What I tell I remember only through God's grace,"[59] Frieda says, as she answers her grandchildren's questions about Canada, the country she left so long ago. Her first-person narrative serves as chorus to the other Mennonites' tales of exile. The reader comes to replace the wide-eyed children clamouring for stories from their *Urgrossmuttchi*, for Frieda's narrative, which continues at four intervals (Chapters i, iii, vi, and x), represents the novel's only unembellished, straightforward revelation of a personal reality. "My Life: That's as It Was" — the common title of each of Frieda's chapters — signals her short, simple style of speaking. Whereas other sections of the novel show more stylistic variation, Frieda Friesen recounts her own past in a manner devoid of sentimentality and nostalgia; hers is a direct, witty recollection of even the most horrid or poignant of events. A refrain echoing the words of her father, Isaak, punctuates each of the sections devoted to her tale: ". . . it does all come from God, strength and sickness, want and plenty" (p. 10). Frieda's is a voice of experience that is refreshing in numerous ways. Her ultimate acceptance of all that befalls her is not without its humour; for instance, of her wedding night she remarks, "Huh, that was a whaling all right" (p. 45), and this winning candidness informs even her less happy moments. The narrative style is an apt rendering of dialect, for the inclusion of German vocabulary and the sometimes awkward grammar make it appear that Frieda is silently translating as she speaks. Her simple declaration "That was a hard time" (p. 92) conjures in understated fashion their early times in Paraguay, when she was burying some of her children, who had died of typhoid, and bearing others. Again, the incredible starkness of "At evening he died" (p. 148), signalling the death of her husband of fifty-four years, is more touching than any amount of lamentation could be. The fearful, demonic South American landscape provides a marked contrast to the Canadian, Russian, and Chinese settings referred to in other narratives. Frieda's last instalment makes a pointed comparison between the world she has fought and subdued and that which she knows she could have had in Canada. She seldom judges, but once back in Canada for a visit, ". . . it was all English and not Mennonite but the most people there came from us and to me it sometimes looked they were stretching themselves around for what they weren't. Maybe they weren't" (p. 149). Despite the appealing frankness of each of Frieda's contributions, though, they seem strangely unsatisfactory in terms of the whole novel.

Even the apparently uncomplicated nature of her particular narratives is deceiving. They represent the one linear aspect of the novel — Frieda narrates the events of her life in chronological order — yet each section remains oddly open-ended, even the final one. In fact, there is no sense of finality in any of the narratives, a characteristic which is normally acceptable in a short story but not in a novel. Wiebe suggests that this is precisely the way of history, and Ina Ferris maintains that such is also the way of art: Wiebe's "antilinearity places in doubt the time structures the human mind erects, particularly that of history, and works to undercut the sense of time as history — the traditional time of the novel as a genre" (Ferris, p. 91). Frieda's first narrative, which is only a few pages in length, describes her young years in Canada, leaving off around the time of her marriage in 1903. The following story, a much longer one, occurs during a few weeks' time in Russia in 1929. Once the narrative is back in Frieda's hands in the third section, the early years of her marriage fly by, and Frieda and her husband are on their 1927 voyage to Paraguay in a matter of a few pages. The fourth chapter is narrated from America in the 1960s but concerns the events of Franz Epp's life in Moscow one evening in 1929. The following section details the flight of Liesel Driediger and others of the Russian Mennonite community in 1930 to Buenos Aires by ship. It is told from her ten-year-old-girl perspective, so that her utter self-absorption and frivolity make for a sharp contrast when Frieda again picks up her own story in the typhus-infested, war-torn wilds of Paraguay. She relates her family's pioneer years there from 1927 to 1934, at which point the narrative shifts to recount her daughter Anna's adventure at the community well. What follows is one night in old Jacob Friesen's march to a labour camp in Siberia. Jacob is referred to in the second and fourth sections of the novel, and finally, in this section, his experience becomes reality.

This continuous juxtaposition of personae, of style, and of narrative stance completely undermines traditional novelistic structure. As the reader becomes increasingly disoriented, individual narratives are apprehended as more immediate; Wiebe insists that every detail be noticed as a highly significant ingredient in the overall panorama of events. Individual chapter titles come to be increasingly emblematic of each character's ordeal; Jacob's unit, entitled "The Cloister of the Lilies," is blackly ironic in terms of what transpires there. But taken in succession, these captions — from "Lilies," through "Drink Ye All of It," "Wash, This Sand and Ashes," and "The Vietnam Call of Samuel U. Reimer," to "On the Way" — provide a larger, more strictly religious perspective, which is the one unifying concept of the novel. The mobile structure of multiperspective and polychronic story is thus as transient as are the wandering Mennonites; in fact, ". . . the novel's central image of journeying stresses process not completion, . . . so the cumulation of the basic narrative units . . . signifies the novel's search for form, translating into narrative terms the existential problems explored in the fiction" (Ferris, pp. 91–92). Wiebe's creation, then, is not only multivoiced on a horizontal plane, it is also multilevelled in a vertical sense. There exist, on a mundane level, the same symbols (mainly religious) and themes that have characterized all of his works; on a more sophisticated level, however, *The Blue Mountains of China* can be considered a treatise evaluating the process of reinterpreting history through art. Where history is usually perceived as a haphazard sequence of events and art as the ultimate principle of order, Wiebe has subverted the former premise to the latter. Once historical continuum is undermined, the only order is art; once that too is disjointed, so are the reader's expectations. *The Blue Mountains of China* is thus a much more organic novel in terms of how it renders life; the moment, even if it is only a remembered one, becomes the one essential thing.

The cinematographic quality of this novel, a quality which also characterizes the later *Temptations of Big Bear* and *The Scorched-Wood People*, is one mark of Wiebe's increasing sophistication as a descriptive writer.[60] There are certain narrative sequences which are so densely and immediately rendered that they conjure up the kind of visual feast usually found only on film. There are numerous luscious moments in "Sons and Heirs," the novel's second section, in which Jacob Friesen the fifth alternately rejects and indulges in his insistent physicality. The mounting rhythm of the prose, as he gives way to his urges, is hypnotic:

> Abrupt behind him on the beat came the finger snap, sharp as bone breaking, and his feet were in syncopation, circling her slowly but faster, body buoyed inevitably by the beat, by the fantastic lifting bass springing under his boot-soles and through each muscle like light, by the swinging gyre of her eyes and arms and hips. (p. 36)

Similarly, in "Black Vulture," Franz Epp's phantasmagorical rendering of events from forty years past is compelling:

> I was hidden in a doorway, the black of it my shelter, but then I was out in the street and I think I fell, screaming, a GPU hand on my shoulder, long roaring happy faces, saucer eyes staring in tears, but there was no one at all on the silent street. Only myself and a foot winding-rag lying on the snow. I was sprawled on the street hammering at the trampled snow in the moonlight with the wall of the Kremlin above me. Maybe screaming too; I don't know. (p. 69)

Powerful images like the winding-rag and the Black Vulture — the demonic Party limousine, which whisks people away never to be heard from again — resonate with all the horror the story has sought to conjure up. They are the novel's filmic elements, brief flashes of which invoke more than each narrator can possibly articulate.

Certain of the narratives are more compelling than others. "Drink Ye All of It," for instance, is one of the most complex sections of *The Blue Mountains of China* precisely because of what it does not say. It contains the novel's title symbol; thankfully, however, the symbol is not belaboured but is evoked only towards the chapter's end. The chapter begins in a third-person narrative voice: "The louse was tight against the skin, blunt feelers motionless" (p. 117). The inhuman objectivity achieved with the use of "the skin" is maintained even when the narrative perspective shifts to an utterly loose, disoriented stream of consciousness:

> *clutched tight   gasps muffled immovable tighter and*
> *tighter to prayers   groaning sleighs in the fantastic it's in-*
> *human cold   enough to split the rigid dead in the cemetery*
> *behind the domed church   worming along . . . o my lovely*
> *quiet quiet and warm under the blankets tight* (pp. 117–18)

Interspersed between dialogue and objective description are snatches from David Epp's thought flow and details from an encyclopaedic entry about the legendary blue mountains the villagers are to cross. Officially, they are *"the Greater Khingan Mountains of China seven hundred miles from the great bend of the Amur River"* (p. 125), but David quietly complements this with his own, disjointed perception of them as *"the thin blue sketch, beckoning from across the river the beautiful mocking blue"* (p. 126). Pieces from the communion service also punctuate that main part of the story in which David inwardly struggles with his moral responsibility towards those of his people left behind. There is no concrete evidence that such will occur, until, near the end, he simply asks his friend Bernhard to take care of his wife, Erna, and their child. What David articulates to his friend is so much less than what he has internally agonized over; Wiebe uses the occasion to probe David's inmost understanding and anguished passion:

> His mind lay open, indefensible as being, churning with every
> one collected thing sharp like a broken tooth yet coated and
> smeared with every other. He knew no formula prayers except
> the to him now useless ones of childhood and he was clutching
> like a sinking man to an endless chain hand over hand that slid
> out at each touch "O dear God my blessed Lord Jesus . . ."
> until it lifted him at last at terrifying last to the inevitable.
> (pp. 131–32)

The pitfalls of translating from German to Russian, portrayed authentically enough, and moments of the bartering session among the Chinese, the Russians, and the Mennonite refugees divert attention from David's impending martyrdom. There is little sense of completion as the camera fades out on David, who is back in the village from which he led his people in escape, sitting "motionless, watching, waiting for the louse to come to his warm flesh" (p. 140). His doom is unspoken, but nonetheless present.

The final chapter, "On the Way," is of a piece with the progressive quality of the novel. It is itself comprised of three subsections, each of which serves to bring together many of the characters introduced earlier. Liesel Driediger is now Dr. Elizabeth Cereno and is forty-eight years of age; she happens upon old Jacob Friesen, who was last seen heading towards a labour camp. Frieda Friesen's daughter Esther and her family also come in for an encore, and all of them converge at the same time in a ditch beside the Trans-Canada Highway near Calgary. The occasion is Canada's centennial year as celebrated by young John Reimer; his cross and his trek across the nation draw attention to his being a Mennonite, and the others flock around him as if to redeem their own lapsed faith. The scene is poignant: each of the characters bears an invisible, but nevertheless heavy, past, except for John and the Williams (formerly Willms) family, and these find it even more difficult to maintain their faith in the plastic, neon world they have helped to create. Nevertheless, this last chapter of *The Blue Mountains of China* is the least successful because it is so didactic. The narrative bogs down when the existential questions that plague each chapter in turn are again relentlessly pursued. All subtlety is lost in the onslaught of confessions and metaphysics and "blue mountains" (p. 227). The brilliance of the mosaic is only momentarily obscured, however, for it is still the lilies, the well, and the putrid decay of an Indian's leg that one remembers.

With *The Temptations of Big Bear*, Wiebe shifts his focus exclusively to the Canadian prairies and the natives who roamed them not so long ago. The novel is composed as a fugue for several narrative voices of different qualities, each of which emphasizes the tension between references to past and present. They lend the story a psychological realism that is more authentic than any social vision could be; the truth, Wiebe contends, must lie somewhere between private consciousness and public declaration.

Wiebe's narrators take their cue from the unforgettable Big Bear. "Words are not just sound . . . ,"[61] he proposes, and the several public and private sensibilities who manipulate language in accordance with the quality of their narrative voice are proof of this. What accounts for the effectiveness of the novel is that Wiebe constantly juxtaposes these voices so that private experience translates public knowledge, and present sensations pass into historical fact. The events from which the common history of Big Bear's people and the white man are woven are consistently seen in duplicate; the omniscient narrator, true to the sacredness of his calling, observes from both within and outside his chosen narrators. This third-person narrative framework boasts various qualities of voice, ranging from a fairly flat, expository style, to a brisk, journalistic account of facts, and even further to a sensual, hypnotic poetry. At times, the narrator lapses into silence: action is surrendered to dialogue, and the novel reads like a drama. Passages in italics denote the invasion of voices from beyond the Indian frame of reference; written documents incarnate for the Indians the voice of the Grandmother (the queen of England), the magical power of the Roman Catholic church, and the strange, rigid decrees of the law. Testimonies from private individuals complete the array of narrative voices; they provide that psychological realism without which *The Temptations of Big Bear* would be just another exercise in mythology.

A voice somewhere between that of the journalist and that of the poet opens the novel; it is the voice which introduces four of the story's six chapters, and, while it remains descriptive, it also frequently displays a dry sense of humour. The land described at the beginning of the action springs to life through the careful manipulation of words:

> The huge river turning past the tiny peaks of the buildings, coils of it spinning in circles like suns, its grey water so thick, so heavy with silt it seemed to bulge up out of its bed, lean against hills. And trees on the diagonal slopes, . . . like spines, . . . poplars and fading yellow birch like sprouting grass impossible to ride through . . . . Who would sign away such land? As if they had a choice. (p. 11)

This level of narrative provides the framework for the story's events. It is presented in this particular instance as an inner meditation of Governor Morris; he proves himself to be sensitive to the phenomena he describes yet incurably subjective. However outwardly well-intentioned, this white narrator must be questioned. The character of Big Bear springs to life in the same way as that of Morris: before becoming a physical reality, it is his voice, "the enormous strange depths of that incomprehensible voice" (p. 19), that defines him. The narrator here is content to remain outside Big Bear; in this case, the narrator's is a private view of a public world.

But this narrative voice is itself multilevelled, and capable of generating a wide variety of effects. Frequently it is oracular, speaking from the past while fully aware of the outcome of what is being described. Yet we are never permitted to forget that the narrator is also human; he frequently allows himself to judge events, thereby adding a certain moral dimension to the novel:

> Not quite $53,000 for a bit more than fifty thousand square miles of grass and hills. A down payment actually, but complete with rivers, valleys, minerals, sky — everything, forever. Rotting buffalo. (p. 69)

Such acerbic wit sets the tone for the entire chapter; not content to simply play the journalist, he must embellish facts with opinion. Again and again, he betrays his unreliability as a reporter; he distorts facts at will in order to provide a story behind the facts — which remains, ironically, the essence of the history.

The narrator bounds from fact to opinion and from present to past without disturbing the fluidity of the story. The reconstruction of the Frog Lake massacre opens with snatches from communiqués between officials, each of which foreshadows, consciously or unconsciously, the coming tragedy. The narrative attempts to sound purely reportorial as it translates private communication into public knowledge. However, the bias is poorly concealed. Following is a quotation from a letter written by Superintendent Crozier:

> It does not seem to me reasonable to expect a lot of pure savages to settle down and become steady farmers all at once . . . . Government policy should be, as it has been in the past, one of conciliation. There is only one other, and that is to fight them. (p. 209)

Here, personal truth is filtered twice before becoming public, first as written by the Superintendent, and again through the ostensible third-person narrator. The narrator effectively manipulates the emotional pitch of the novel; during this chapter especially, switching from the past to the present and back again effects a steady increase in the rhythm and tension of events.

It is this more obvious, omniscient narrator's unbridled flights into sensuous, poetic language that dominate. Offering only glimpses of his capabilities, he frequently undermines the beauty of one vision with the hopelessly sordid language of another, similar vision. Witness young Kingbird's sexual experience with the mare:

> Gently, slowly he felt the tension build in him like a bow bending to the pull; his whole body drawing forward into the anticipation of his hands as they gradually and unceasingly moved and he felt the mare as if broadening under his left hand, seeming to lower herself and spread wider, slacker till the muscles under her skin seemed to shimmer over blood singing as his right moved ever higher . . . . [His] right fingers brushed a damp fold, slipped, . . . plunging by a membrane with a brush softer than sweet-grass down into a hot, boundless, swirling swamp. The mare screamed brilliantly. (pp. 54–55)

At once inside and outside the sensibility of Kingbird, the increasing tension of the language accompanies the urgency of the experience. There is little or no distance between physical and psychological experience in the Indian; Kingbird's motions are closely attuned to his senses, and his whole being throbs with life. Here, social realism is subordinate to private vision; the facts behind the history recede, and individual consciousness is all. Such moments are fleeting, but their vitality invests the novel with uncommon poetic vigour. This effect is shattered soon after when the sound of grunting draws Kingbird onto a scene of humans copulating. Beauty and mystery are lost in banal language, and the narrative slips back into the hands of the placid journalist.

Vigorous writing, however, is at its peak in incomparable passages of pure stream of consciousness. Wiebe abandons himself to beautiful lyrics, which serve to suspend the characters in time and lull the reader into a false sense of security. History and race are forgotten in the now, and for John Delaney and Sits Green On The Earth, the now is eternal:

> They were no hail mary or agnus dei overlearned thoughtless slaver but a slimed thoughtless unyoking of 'unbridled liberty' — YES — 'unbridled liberty' from nails and knobs and slivers of the cross, of clenched lips and clenched legs propriety, of

god's beard and fundament aylmer ontario, of pawing though
the wounds and private pricks of jesus shriveled against wood,
exploding breasts lank as needles . . . . (p. 232)

John Delaney's flow of consciousness fashions a release, an escape
from convention, out of the moan that identifies Sits Green On The
Earth. She is the "soft blot in the bowl under the spruce that could
swallow him into eternal resting oblivion" (p. 233); in him, past
merges with present experience, the thought process is sacrificed to
the senses, and his consciousness runs rampant. At no time is moral
judgement imposed on the action; the action simply occurs. The
effect is an almost surrealistic intensification of private reality;
Wiebe's characters live in every dimension, and their adventures
demand the reader's vicarious participation.

Wiebe also attempts to distort this main narrative voice by occasionally adopting that of a fairly artificial narrator. At various points
in the novel, italics represent the incarnation of white man's law, the
Roman Catholic church, and the queen, more affectionately known
as the Grandmother. These intrusions are all courtesy of the white
man and remain menacing reminders for the Indian that their time of
buffalo hunting is limited:

> *NOW THIS INSTRUMENT WITNESSETH, that the said "Big Bear,"*
> *for himself and on behalf of the Band which he represents, does*
> *transfer, surrender and relinquish to Her Majesty the Queen . . .*
> *all his right, title and interest whatsoever, which he has held or*
> *enjoyed, of, in and to the territory described and fully set out in*
> *the treaty . . . .* (p. 132)

The voice of the white queen is characteristically impersonal and
rigid, as is that of the white man's law: "And further (etc.) . . . to wit,
on the 17th day of April in the year aforesaid and on divers other days
and times, as well before as after that day, at or near the locality
known as Fort Pitt (etc.) . . ." (p. 353). How sterile and petty is the
speech assigned to the white man! Only in religious matters does
language thaw at all: *"Glory . . . God on high, and on earth peace
. . ."* (p. 250). Even here, though, the language spoken is not English
but Latin. Only with the Indian does the voice spring from the self.
Witness Big Bear's terrifying song: "my teeth are my knives / my
claws are my knives" (p. 182). Again, these are contrived distortions

of the main narrative frame; while infrequent and brief, they are clues to the mutual distrust between Indians and whites.

In addition to the anonymous official voices, there exists a cast of about eight private, or individual, narrators, each of whom, with the exception of Big Bear, represents a strictly white point of view. A religious outlook is characterized in the voice of missionary John McDougall, politics has its say through Indian Affairs Commissioner Edgar Dewdney, and the military point of view is presented by the Canadian Volunteer. The rest of the chorus is made up of characters such as Robert Jefferson, the farm instructor, Mrs. Delaney and George Stanley, both settlers, and Big Bear himself. Each narrative voice is true to the character from whom it issues, and the most outstanding example of this occurs in the journal of Kitty McLean. Here are the perceptions of the young woman who is yet a child:

> Papa said an Indian captive had to supply himself, though I never noticed that in the books I read. Food usually appeared there without the least worry by the heroine, though she could rarely eat any and was always perfectly clean and disdainful and aloof about the fate worse than death suspended over her head . . . . (p. 272)

Oddly enough, she is one of the few white people in the novel who recognizes the encompassing vision of Big Bear. She idolizes him, and he in turn acknowledges a kindred spirit in her. In one of the most stirring passages in the novel, these two come together under the power of the sun. Race fades as Kitty acquiesces to his wisdom:

> She felt herself becoming again, the farthest tips of her moving out towards fire until she knew herself too complete to comprehend, too enormous, each unknown part of her vastness she could not yet quite feel but which would certainly surround the whole earth bending back under her. (p. 314)

Most of the other individual narrators do not respond to events with the same immediacy; to a large extent, their stories are exercises in memory, in the sense that events are related from the point of view of someone who already knows what the outcome will be. Again, there is the imposition of a double vision, of which even the characters themselves are not conscious; indeed, it is triple vision when the main filtering device is considered.

Whatever the major differences between the two conflicting cultures may be, Wiebe is intent on demonstrating that they do have something in common after all. This must be their sense of the past — a shared past — rooted in the land on which it occurred. As far as the Indian is concerned, land cannot be owned: "No one can choose for only himself a piece of the Mother Earth. She is. And she is for all that live, alike . . . . Who can receive land? From whom would he receive it?" (pp. 28–29). In this lies the basic dissension between white man and Indian, and it is propagated because neither comprehends the implications informing the language of the other.

The Temptations of Big Bear confines in written language a tradition that has, until this time, been verbal. The sense of history Wiebe evokes plumbs the depths of many a private consciousness, resulting in a montage of individual impressions. The various narrative levels are what give credence to this "pastness of the past," and the quality of language assigned to each determines the degree to which the past informs the present. Hence a more personal than public vision of Big Bear and the events surrounding his dispossession informs our perception of him. As a victim, he certainly inspires respect and sympathy, but his native nobility discourages pity. The portrayal of his character succeeds because he is not impervious to the lessons of time; caught in a vise between memories of the plenitude of the past and realities of the paucity of the present, he accepts with gratitude his time to die.

Some important short stories spring out of the periods during which Wiebe was wrestling with *The Temptations of Big Bear* and, later, with *The Scorched-Wood People*. Such notable pieces as "Where Is the Voice Coming From?" (1971), "Along the Red Deer and the South Saskatchewan" (1973), and "Games for Queen Victoria" (1976) embody perhaps even more fully than *The Temptations of Big Bear* and *The Scorched-Wood People* Wiebe's artistic philosophy about evolving "story" from the "finite acts, . . . orders, . . . elemental feelings and reactions, . . . [and] obvious legal restrictions and requirements"[62] of historical fact. "Story *is*, much longer than the fact," contends Wiebe (*SM*, p. xi).

A successful irony pervades "Where Is the Voice Coming From?"; Wiebe, the would-be interpreter of dry, static details into living art, must first come to terms with the demands of time. Wiebe suggests that, like Michelangelo, the storyteller releases the story from the "encumbering rock" ("On the Trail," p. 133) of facts around it. By resurrecting the original story from historical realities that only weigh it down, Wiebe feels he is simply maintaining that tradition of telling and retelling by which the story gains warmth and immediacy: ". . . the so-called lies — the accretions and deletions of each new telling — are more humanly significant than literal facts can ever be . . . . The 'lies' of good stories are always, perversely, truer than 'facts.'"[63] A reliance on the concrete can tyrannize the creative writer who seeks to be more true to the essence of history than to the letter of it. Official data is never hard to find. In a museum, for instance, Wiebe can easily detail what remains of Almighty Voice: "The first item to be seen is the piece of white bone. It is almost triangular, slightly convex . . ." ("Where," p. 136). But bone does not speak; or rather, it does, but it depends who is listening.

The picture of Almighty Voice somehow does not correspond to the facts of his physical description. What Wiebe sees is not what officialdom has told him, and he recognizes that were he to depend solely upon precise details, his creativity would soon flounder. In "Bear Spirit in a Strange Land," Wiebe describes his apprehension at being, finally, so close to the spirit of Big Bear: "As I touch that [his power bundle] I should feel something: . . . something for my own apprehension of wanting to see this, to somehow *have* this like any white who never has enough, of anything, as if it were even possible to actually have enough of anything except within yourself."[64] He quails similarly when confronting a photograph of Almighty Voice, because ". . . even in this watered-down reproduction of unending reproductions of that original, a steady look into those eyes cannot be endured. It is a face like an axe" ("Where," p. 141). Even in death, the Indian sends forth a wordless challenge to the writer; no longer does anything move on the poplar bluff where Almighty Voice last fought, yet that land endures. Wiebe will be as happily inexact about Gitchie-Manitou Wayo as he cares to be, for details are never important. "I could be more accurate if I had a reliable interpreter who would make a reliable interpretation. For I do not, of course, understand the Cree myself" ("Where," p. 143). No matter; only a devotion to the spirit of the people of the past is essential.

In "Along the Red Deer and the South Saskatchewan," Little Bear relates an account of the attempted massacre, under the leadership of his beloved Appino-kommit, of a band of Plains Cree. The story was originally translated by F. W. Spicer; it thus comes to us at two removes from the original. But, as W. J. Keith points out, Wiebe has, in fact, rescued the original from the melodramatic and sentimental clichés of Spicer's version.[65] The first, glorious moments of the attack are recreated — rather than simply recounted — "in the rhythms and modulations of the prose."[66] Witness this historical reinterpretation of a vibrant moment in a young warrior's life:

> . . . lodges split themselves before our sharp knives and the enemy staggers out, snatching at weapons and falling, snatching and falling and trying to stand zipp! Arrows hiss some of us down but who sees that, we are forcing them back, they are summer flies, their clubs and knives just flies brushed aside and crushed I yo ho the joy of knife thudding in bone and blood spray . . . .[67]

Once the battle turns to nightmare for his band, Little Bear intones the litany of the devastation in similarly effective language. The defeat matures him like no success in battle could have, for, as a survivor, it is his duty to reveal the names of the massacred. "Friend, can you know how I felt? Do you know pain? That was what made us men, then, such happiness and such pain . . . . Our hearts had to know and hold both . . . ."[68] Wiebe's invisible narrative presence puts us face to face with Little Bear as his questions leap out to drive us from mere disinterestedness.

"Games for Queen Victoria" is a masterly recreation of an incident not included in *The Scorched-Wood People*. To Wiebe, the game of billiards played at Fort Garry prior to the arrival of Wolseley in 1870 is emblematic of all that led to Riel's downfall in 1885. The many references to games in the story culminate in the description of William F. Butler's one-man onslaught on a billiard table:

> It seemed my hands played a delicate machine, a lock, perhaps, whose tumblers clicked into place wherever my hand moved; I saw each shot immediately, my legs moved, my hands made each exact stroke as if propelled by a power beyond their own. Finally, I had made a particularly intricate two-bank play . . . when I sensed I must pass two moccasined feet at the corner of the billiard table. They belonged to a stocky man in formal

black trousers and coat, sallow, puffy face, and large head, whose square-cut, massive forehead was overhung by thickly clustered hair — altogether a remarkable face driven almost to hypnosis by glaring black eyes.[69]

The apparition is Riel himself, of course, and the utter distance between the two cultures is never more apparent than when the incongruously black-trousered and moccasined figure attempts to communicate with that suave, utterly British efficiency and arrogance represented by Butler. Riel's philosophy of peace and brotherhood does not impress Butler: "Half the New World," Butler laments, "and he [Riel] could only mewl over the bits of blood it would cost . . . . He must have read the disappointment on my face. Undoubtedly even my disgust at the meanness of his ambition."[70] This white man persistently underestimates Riel's legendary stature; like other colonizers, Butler cannot see beyond his visitor's incongruous garb, a short-sightedness that will cost the white settlers dearly. If that particular part of the West's history is beyond the confines of this particular story, it is no matter: history fills in the blank. Wiebe, again the indiscernible third-person narrator, distils a minor incident trapped in the annals of time into a moment of revelation.

Pierre Falcon, prime narrator and master of ceremonies in *The Scorched-Wood People*, provides a much more sympathetic view of this religious and political leader of the Métis. The novel is comprised of four parts, each of which bears a title relating directly to the action it details; thus, "Riel's Province" discusses the making of the Provisional Government, "Wilderness" deals with Riel's exile in the States, "Gabriel's Army" describes the failure of the 1885 rebellion, and "Riel and Gabriel" serves as an epilogue and tribute to the martyred Riel. The overall structure of the novel proves to be circular: the first section begins where the third part finishes. The novel begins as a flashback to November 1869; Riel is carefully dressing himself in front of a mirror in Fort Garry, just prior to the celebration of the First Provisional Government of Red River. From the next room, he hears the sound of laughter. Pierre Falcon, narrating in retrospect, knows that sixteen years later, Riel

will hear only his own feet slur a steady prayer down the corridor, moving him to the wood he has heard them hammering together on the prairie outside his window, to steps he will obediently mount while a bulging sun burns the hoar-frost into sheet gold; there to be hanged by his neck until he is at last, perfectly, dead. O my God have mercy.[71]

The end, then, is inevitable. Since the narrative is circular, we know from the beginning how the story will end; by repeating the description of Riel dressing himself, Falcon frustrates our desire for suspense and concentrates our attention on this last, banal act of a most inspired man. Hence, on the day he is hanged — Tuesday, 10 November 1885 — Riel "was dressing himself, carefully. And he remembered that dressing in Fort Garry . . ." (p. 344). The scene darkens as Riel, "his own feet slurring a steady prayer down the corridor" (p. 344), goes to his death. Falcon reminds us time and again of the impending doom of many characters. He quells at the outset our addiction to plot and strives to direct attention to his words, to his songs and prayers — that is, to the essence of his narrative.

Wiebe views the Métis in much the same way as he views the Mennonites in *The Blue Mountains of China*. He sees their quest for selfhood as part of a much larger, ongoing process. To Wiebe, history is itself cyclical, and he presents histories within the greater pattern as also cyclical; hence the Métis's implicit belief in Riel's eventual resurrection. Allan Dueck points out that "the larger pattern of Wiebe's novels is always a clue to their meaning."[72] The prologues to the two acts of Métis defiance, during 1869–70 and again in 1885, are identical, Dueck notes. "The twice-repeated cycle of Métis experience gives way only in the promise of a third cycle through the person of Louis Riel, who, as the novel's ending affirms, may become the voice for new life."[73] On the proverbial third day, as both Dumont and Falcon optimistically intimate, the spirit of Riel will rise again to deliver the people of the *bois-brûlés*. Of what occurs until such time, Falcon "cannot sing . . . . Eighty years later they [the Métis] would be known simply as 'road allowance people,' having no place whatever except in their clanking wagons, their rusted cars on the placeless public roads. In his stifling summer cell Riel saw this coming horror . . . . For his visions did not stop" (p. 328). Again, all conjectures, judgements, and facts are related in retrospect, and the sense of cyclicality in progress constantly informs the narrative structure.

How Falcon, born in 1793, can relate what he does — he even

includes observations on the twentieth-century plight of the Métis —
demonstrates a remarkable narrative feat. His is the ostensible third-
person point of view from which all is detailed. As Riel's grandfather,
Falcon inspires confidence even if his historical presence is unveri-
fiable. But then, for Wiebe, such is insignificant anyway. What is
most convincing about Falcon's narrative voice is simply that it
springs from a heritage that is also Riel's:

> That's just how it is, a people with two heritages so rich that
> often one alone is more than you want, when you feel one of
> them move in you like a living beast and the other whispers,
> sings between your ears with a beauty you would gladly sell
> your soul to hear until you die. Such doubleness, such some-
> times half-and-half richness of nothing. (p. 112)

Not only, then, does the old Métis provide factual renderings of
occurrences, he also dictates an entire historical and social perspective. Falcon is never shy about probing the depths of minds like Riel's
and Dumont's, nor is he ever remiss in offering conjectures or self-
righteous judgements on the events he relates. Further, Falcon
reveals a powerful eye for the dramatic, and his language exhibits a
remarkable diversity of tone and style. He is the poet-singer of his
people; communication means everything to Falcon, and it is this
that he shares with Riel. In fact, since Riel comes to be identified with
David, the Israelite poet-king, Falcon can be seen to recount the life
of a fellow artist.

Riel's weapons are sharpened by education, ambition, and vision;
he is the religious and political leader of the Métis, and Falcon
remains the articulator of their ethnic spirit. While Riel's language is
religious, Falcon's is not. Only when he is inside Riel, witnessing
visions through Riel's eyes, does his secular perspective expand to
accommodate the private, more intense experiences which feed
Riel's ambition. Moments in which the narrative voice is neither
simply Riel's nor Falcon's, but both, remain the most powerful in the
novel.

Germane to accepting Falcon's version of events preceding and
including the 1885 rebellion is a belief in Falcon, on the part of the
reader, as intense as Falcon's faith in Riel. Falcon's method of
garnering information is easy because, as he explains, great men
simply do not know he exists: ". . . they never protected themselves

from my thoughts . . . . Let me tell you immediately, Louis Riel was a giant. If God had willed it, he could have ruled the world. No, no, hear me out, and you will believe it too" (pp. 35–36). The narrator's implicit trust in Riel's mission for the Métis infuses every statement he makes with a vitality that cannot be resisted. To read Falcon is to read Riel is to believe in him also. Of course, the narrative is biased, but this is precisely Wiebe's aim: "The whole point," says Wiebe, "is to give readers a sense and understanding of history from a biased point of view. It doesn't help to be accurate to the historical facts as we know them. What is important is to understand the people that were here before us."[74] Falcon calculates the effect that certain episodes will exert and judiciously presents the most memorable. Technically, he is a filtering device releasing from the tyranny of time an already well-embedded myth. He reinterprets the legend in the light of personal experience and remains entirely credible.

Falcon's versatility is his most appealing trait as narrator. Despite the fact that he is himself an anachronism, historically speaking, he makes certain everything he relates is chronologically accurate. His expertise as a storyteller comes naturally; unencumbered by the sophistication Riel has achieved as a student in Montreal, Falcon is closer to the primitive zest of his people. Snatches of diverse narrative modes embellish the tale, yet all are carefully chosen to illumine some facet of his people's life. For instance, he vividly recounts Dumont's pursuit of McDougall as if it were a buffalo hunt, then he modifies his style to illustrate the white man's obsession with language: ". . . McDougall, like any paper man, hadn't heard a word; he was too busy thinking about his own words pondered so long, written so carefully; he was plowing through the snow to throw the weight of his paper into the case and thereby prove once and for all everything that had to be proved" (p. 16). Later, Falcon turns this incident into a song of celebration for the new Métis government.

In this particular domain, though, the hand of Wiebe, the ultimate narrator, is somewhat more apparent. Falcon shows a real distrust for words, "those detached, dead sounds" (p. 211), especially as wielded by the white man. Yet it is exactly in this white-man way that Riel seeks to emancipate his people from the tyranny of the Hudson's Bay Company and of Ottawa:

And he was writing; words to fill the leather suitcase, to give his unwritten people a place on paper before the frozen earth closed them away one by one and no one would hear them, the words they cried to each other lost like the cry of gulls turning trackless over the river, words to be used against him, for every written word called to judgement. (p. 245)

Riel's obsession with naming, or identifying, the Métis is shared by Falcon, although Falcon would deny it. So too is it ultimately Wiebe's objective; as he has himself proposed, "the essence of language is naming . . . ."[75] The spirit of the Métis rests in the songs of Falcon and thus in an oral tradition; narrator Falcon translates this essence into written form seemingly despite his natural inclination.

Grandfather Falcon proves to be something of a poet; in language close to his own experience, he brings out the essential sensitivity of the Métis towards the land they inhabit: "Under the dead blue sunlight of winter the white prairie always moved, its surface wandering like sand in search of obstacle; slipping over the glazed, or granular, or shadowed levels always forward, always steadily east" (p. 49). It is frequently possible to further discern the influence of Falcon the dramatist, as, when recording a debate among the leaders of the North-West government, he inserts: "(Loud laughter.) . . . (Laughter and cheers)" (p. 63). At times he also plays the journalist; for instance, the unfolding of the story of Thomas Scott's execution takes place as a conversation — almost an interview — between Falcon and Murdock MacLeod. As defender of this Métis decision, which enraged Ottawa and Upper Canada, Falcon is required to dodge the arrows of contention MacLeod hurls at him. But the balanced view he presents of the discussion — even though its effect is calculated to win sympathy for the Métis — further ingratiates this intrepid narrator with his audience.

The style of language Falcon uses varies with his diverse modes of communication. There are many examples of his humorous renderings of events. Usually Falcon exhibits a rather homespun sense of the wry: "What human being likes to hear he has been sold by someone he will never see, so he can never kick him where it will do the longest good?" (p. 29). Falcon also endows much of the novel with a lush, cinematographic quality. The highly emotional reunion of Riel and Dumont reveals an extremely sensitive camera eye:

In the churchyard, the seven-fanned pattern of Bird Tail Rock brilliant in sunlight beyond them, four riders on worn horses.

Buffalo-hide jackets: Métis hunters, rifles strapped to saddles for a long ride. He stood on the log step a moment, the bright world turning into premonition as though he had looked beyond the transparent blue-and-orange-rimmed globe behind his own eyelids; but one broad rider had swung down, was coming toward him in the wide-legged roll of a horseman, and his heart leaped before his mind could name this man . . . .
(p. 181)

Falcon is at his best, though, when he is least evident. There are a few moments in both Riel's and Dumont's lives in which they experience a transcendental vision of otherness. When Falcon can so tap into a consciousness that narrator and character become indistinguishable, then his language is most poetic:

. . . the fire . . . raged in double spires, bits floating away in flames, a cathedral blazing to its two gigantic crosses tilting toward each other in the relentless slow motion of melting into themselves though their bells tolled on, closer and closer, as if the fire intensified their thunder, and through their tolling the flames spoke to him in a voice he had heard, o he had heard . . . . He tore his aching bones away, flames burst like flowers over his body and he roared with them, a rolling sun of fire. (p. 95)

Falcon's language, then, swings from the merely documentary — as when providing certain medical opinions on the question of Riel's sanity — to the idiom of prayer, and further to the rhetoric of politics as wielded by the likes of Macdonald and Riel. He is at his acerbic best when defending Riel:

I have often felt the CPR might at least have named a hotel after Riel; at the very least given him what they gave Father Lacombe for the relatively puny service of talking Crowfoot out of a railroad right-of-way across the Blackfoot Reserve: a life-time train pass. But I'm being peevish, I suppose. (p. 247)

His utter devotion to Riel is expressed nowhere better than when he describes an incident just prior to the final rebellion. Riel has just baptized a man in front of all the Métis and horrified priests:

Sixty-seven years later Jaxon would die a pauper on the side-walk in front of the New York hotel that had expelled him . . . . Sometimes, when I think of him and the happiness that this moment on his knees gave him in a life much too long with sickness and rejection, I believe I could accept losing my family and all those years far from my place and people . . . if I had one such memory. (p. 225)

Wiebe endows Falcon with licence far exceeding the role of a mere recording device; he is the spirit of his people and freely interprets and judges occurrences from his all-inclusive viewpoint. There is nothing sacred to Falcon; he even follows Louis and Marguerite into their bedroom. But it is a necessary and totally effective liberty. The only important thing, according to Wiebe, is to expand our aware-ness of time to include a living past. Why search for an exclusively Canadian identity when it already exists?

Wiebe's continuing endeavours to unearth the secrets of the West have led to the publication of his one dramatic attempt, *Far as the Eye Can See*. He collaborated with Theatre Passe Muraille to pro-duce a script complete with a wise old Indian, Princess Louise and her Regal Dead, farmers, engineers for Calgary Power, and, cer-tainly not least, Peter Lougheed as the guest *deus ex machina*. The action centres on the attempt by Calgary Power to expropriate farmers' land for a power-plant project and on how this invasion will affect the farmers, natives, and townspeople involved. Princess Louise's hysterics are part of the reason for the play's at times turgid dialogue. Still, there are some ironic moments, such as the final one between Crowfoot and Lougheed:

Crowfoot: A hundred years ago the white man took this country, and now they know the black burning stone is under the earth; and they will not be able to leave it alone. White men can never leave, anything, the way it was.

Lougheed: We have listened to you and we have understood you. Thank you.[76]

Far more successful is Wiebe's short-story accompaniment to the photographic panorama of *Alberta: A Celebration*. The fourteen stories, many of which Wiebe discovered and retold in his own fashion, span even more than the seventy-five years of Alberta's provincehood. Among the better tales are "After Thirty Years of Marriage" — settling the land from a woman's point of view — and "The Year We Gave Away the Land," which deals in true Wiebe style with Indian concessions to the demands of the white man. This collection is more than the coffee-table volume some critics saw it as.

Wiebe's vigour as myth maker proved unabated with the appearance of *The Mad Trapper*, which elaborates on the life of the Rat River trapper Albert Johnson. The novel is a linear, fast-paced narrative depicting a series of confrontations between the RCMP and the madman who refuses to be named. Once he is labelled, Johnson leads the Mounties on an incredible chase over impossible terrain, killing as he goes. The adventure is related skilfully, and the mystery of the mad trapper remains intact. But dialogue and characterization simply do not bear comparison with Wiebe's two preceding novels. Neither Wop May's bitterness nor Spike Millen's fatal fascination with Johnson is adequately evolved, although Johnson's monomania is well portrayed:

> When the blizzard staggered, momentarily eddied into daylight and, as it seemed, caught its breath, he would sometimes glance up to see the peaks about him: the enormous vista of groaning, moving snow, the ravines and ice-blasted pyramids that howled dolefully as the blizzard shook itself and howled, howled. But he did not stop; he forced himself steadily ahead, upwards. If he ever stopped moving in that inhuman lethal world, he would never move again.[77]

As always, it is Wiebe's evocation of the land that proves most effective.

The Angel of the Tar Sands and Other Stories, published in 1982, is really a Collected Stories. All sixteen tales have previously appeared elsewhere, and certainly all Wiebe's "greatest hits" are here. Some, like "The Good Maker," have seen print in less familiar places like *The Mennonite Brethren Herald*, so it is a pleasure to find them here. There are no surprises: these stories are united by Wiebe's abiding interests and passions — the land, the natives, the past, love, and language are all given voice. "The Good Maker," for example, finds Wiebe the artist dedicated to reuniting sign with signified, and word with thing:

Man names things. It's his first act as a maker, he makes names for everything around him and while he is doing so he discovers, he understands something profound about himself and his world: there is no partner fit for him. Words are man's creative acts, with them he gains knowledge and understanding. Words, language, that's the highest achievement of man. With a good word I make the best thing I can make, and with a bad word I destroy the best thing.[78]

From the pithy, moving account of settling the prairie in "After Thirty Years of Marriage" to the whimsical/mystical "The Angel of the Tar Sands," this collection provides a solid, worthwhile introduction to Wiebe's fictional concerns. Regrettably, there is no new material.

At first, Wiebe's seventh novel seems a departure from his propensity for historical fiction. While *My Lovely Enemy* is still concerned with themes like man's place in a decidedly Canadian space and time, Wiebe's presentation of them here proves startlingly new.

Edmonton and nearby Vulcan provide the setting for this tripartite novel. More specifically, much of the action occurs in the Micromaterials Reading Room in the library basement at the University of Alberta. Professor James Dyck frequently cloisters himself there in order to root among musty microfiches for information on nineteenth-century Western Canadian Indian and fur-trade history. Dr. Dyck is forty-two, happily married to lovely, Swedish Liv, and father to a dynamic ten-year-old named Becca. Suddenly, gorgeous, dark-maned Gillian enters his life. She is married to boring old Harold Lemming — who is also, incidentally, a professor of history at the university — but they seem to share a blessedly open concept of marriage. With scarcely a whimper, James is drawn into the affair of his life.

James's first-person narrative controls the novel's first section, or fully two-thirds of the book. The second part is but a page long; it bridges Parts I and III and is entitled, aptly enough, "The Black Bridge." The third-person narrator introduced here reacquaints us in the final section with the major characters. Each of Parts I and III is subdivided into chapters identified by number and by month. The action begins with the affair in Edmonton during May and ends with a death and Lazarus-like rebirth near Vulcan in September.

Though we only gradually learn all there is to know about James, we rather quickly grasp what there is to Gillian. She appears incredibly smart, entirely witty, and unbelievably beautiful. Her role is to seduce unsuspecting James and to spar with him on subjects mostly theological. Liv fares little better; we only garner that she works as a travel agent and that at forty she is still fiery and attractive. Liv, too, jousts with James about God and reveals a strong feminist bias when it comes to His gender. Becca asks all the right questions at all the right times; even Tolstoi the dog seems as canine as he can be. James's strong-willed mother, Ruth, and his long-dead, hated father prove to be much more interesting, and more fully realized, characters. Describing old-country *émigrés* is what Wiebe does well.

Jasch, as James is called by his mother, is the first of many children born in Canada following her escape from Russia. His father is rigid and domineering, and Jasch runs away at the age of sixteen. Once his father is dead, he returns to Vulcan to visit his mother and their old family friend Olena. As historian, Professor James Dyck constantly seeks to reaffirm his own and his family's place in a particular past, even while he combs the same geographical location for clues to the past of the land and its original inhabitants. Again, history is both personal and public.

James Dyck proves we are all historians. Whether delving into others' pasts or our own, we are inevitably making history in a never-present now. And one man's history is another man's story. As James focuses specifically on the tale of one Cree chief named Maskepetoon, his own past slowly surfaces. His becomes a modern man's quest for God. Unfortunately, the affair with Gillian seems to encumber, rather than facilitate, the search.

Structurally the novel is cyclical. The first section opens with James's explanation of why he chooses to work in deep, dark library vaults. The final part, narrated in an objective voice, depicts James and Liv and Harold and Gillian descending into the bowels of the earth for a weekend at a very exclusive resort called The Mine. Thus entombed, they achieve a figurative kind of death. Finally, the novel comes full circle with the real death and rebirth of Ruth.

Stylistically *My Lovely Enemy* is uneven. The debates about God and religion between James and his women invariably prove tedious. Dialogue between him and Gillian seems especially forced. Frequently, too, James's digressions are just plain boring; one finds oneself wishing for the least glint of irony to relieve one's impatience with his musings. But if dialogue sometimes sags, at other times, dialect is delightful. Wiebe renders beautifully the use of English as a second language by Mennonites and Indians. For instance, language is never more poignant or powerful than when James converses with his ageing mother. The inclusion of other genres such as poetry and history proves effective in relieving some of the more stagnant sections, and those moments when James's jealousy flares up provide some hilarity. Finally, the sex scenes between Gillian and James — once the two characters finish theologizing, that is — are very erotic and worth waiting for. *My Lovely Enemy*, compelling and frustrating at the same time, provides few clues to the direction Wiebe's next fiction will take.

For a novelist whose career began with a pedestrian formula for writing, Wiebe has evolved an utterly unique style. He has succeeded in reconciling diverse literary bents with his decidedly Christian world view and in wresting for himself a prominent place as a Prairie writer. The refining of narrative technique, a delving ever deeper into the real, shared past of the prairies, and an intense commitment to certain themes have defined Wiebe's increasingly sophisticated fiction. Mostly though, the as yet unarticulated secrets of the land are what inspire his writing. The land itself has no need of definition, but we do; unless familiarized for us by the talent of such as Rudy Wiebe, landscape remains inscrutable and threatening. It is a vast repository of clues as to where we have come from and, hence, where we are going. The land speaks, and Wiebe listens.

NOTES

[1] Rudy Wiebe, "A Novelist's Personal Notes on Frederick Philip Grove," *University of Toronto Quarterly*, 47 (Spring 1978), 189–99; rpt. in *A Voice in the Land: Essays by and about Rudy Wiebe*, ed. W. J. Keith, Western Canadian Literary Documents, No. 2 (Edmonton: NeWest, 1981), p. 217. All further references to this work ("A Novelist's") appear in the text.

[2] Rudy Wiebe, "Tombstone Community," *Mennonite Life*, 19, No. 4 (Oct. 1964), 150–53; rpt. in Keith, ed., *A Voice in the Land*, pp. 19–20, 21.

[3] "Scrapbook" was originally published as "The Midnight Ride of an Alberta Boy," *Liberty*, 33 (Sept. 1956), 22, 64, 66; rpt. (rev.) in *Where Is the Voice Coming From?* (Toronto: McClelland and Stewart, 1974), pp. 13–18.

[4] Donald Cameron, "Rudy Wiebe: The Moving Stream Is Perfectly at Rest," in *Conversations with Canadian Novelists* (Toronto: Macmillan,

1973), Pt. II, p. 148.

⁵ Ken Adachi, "Unusual Author Lives a Life of Christian Example," *The Toronto Star*, 4 Nov. 1977, Sec. D, p. 10.

⁶ Cameron, pp. 156–57.

⁷ George Melnyk, "The Western Canadian Imagination: An Interview with Rudy Wiebe," *Canadian Fiction Magazine*, No. 12 (Winter 1974), pp. 29–34; rpt. in Keith, ed., *A Voice in the Land*, p. 204. All further references to this work (Melnyk) appear in the text.

⁸ David L. Jeffrey, "Biblical Hermeneutic and Family History in Contemporary Canadian Fiction: Wiebe and Laurence," *Mosaic*, 11, No. 3 (Spring 1978), 87–106.

⁹ Rudy Wiebe, "Passage by Land," *Canadian Literature*, No. 48 (Spring 1971), pp. 26–27.

¹⁰ Rudy Wiebe, "On the Trail of Big Bear," *Journal of Canadian Fiction*, 3, No. 2 (1974), 45–48; rpt. in Keith, ed., *A Voice in the Land*, p. 134. All further references to this work ("On the Trail") appear in the text.

¹¹ Eli Mandel, "Where the Voice Comes From" [interview], CBC *The Arts in Review*, 7 Dec. 1974; printed (rev.) in *Quill & Quire*, Dec. 1974, pp. 4, 20; rpt. in Keith, ed., *A Voice in the Land*, p. 153.

¹² Rudy Wiebe, Introd., *The Story-Makers: A Selection of Modern Short Stories*, ed. Rudy Wiebe (Toronto: Macmillan, 1970), p. xiii. In all further references, this work is abbreviated as *SM*.

¹³ Stephen Scobie, "For Goodness' Sake," *Books in Canada*, Feb. 1980, p. 3.

¹⁴ Scobie, p. 5.

¹⁵ Mandel, p. 152.

¹⁶ Rudy Wiebe, "Western Canadian Fiction: Past and Future," *Western American Literature*, 6 (Spring 1971), 29.

¹⁷ Rudy Wiebe, "The Year of the Indian," rev. of *Across the Medicine Line*, by C. Frank Turner, *Wilderness Man*, by Lovat Dickson, and *Gone Indian*, by Robert Kroetsch, *Dalhousie Review*, 54 (Spring 1974), 164.

¹⁸ Rudy Wiebe, Introd., *Stories from Pacific and Arctic Canada*, ed. Rudy Wiebe and Andreas Schroeder (Toronto: Macmillan, 1974), p. 203.

¹⁹ Rudy Wiebe, "Songs of the Canadian Eskimo," *Canadian Literature*, No. 52 (Spring 1972), p. 60.

²⁰ H. R. Percy, rev. of *Peace Shall Destroy Many*, *Canadian Author & Bookman*, 38, No. 2 (Winter 1962), 16.

²¹ S. E. Read, "The Storms of Change," rev. of *Peace Shall Destroy Many*, *Canadian Literature*, No. 16 (Spring 1963), p. 76.

²² F. W. Watt, rev. of *Peace Shall Destroy Many*, in "Letters in Canada

1962: Fiction," *University of Toronto Quarterly*, 32 (July 1963), 400.

²³ Elmer F. Suderman, "Universal Values in Rudy Wiebe's *Peace Shall Destroy Many*," *Mennonite Life*, 20, No. 4 (Oct. 1965), 172–76; rpt. in Keith, ed., *A Voice in the Land*, pp. 69–78.

²⁴ William H. New, *Articulating West: Essays on Purpose and Form in Modern Canadian Literature*, Three Solitudes: Contemporary Literary Criticism in Canada, No. 1 (Toronto: new, 1972), p. 160.

²⁵ Frank Davey, "Rudy Wiebe," in *From There to Here: A Guide to English-Canadian Literature since 1960* (Erin, Ont.: Porcépic, 1974), p. 265.

²⁶ J. M. Stedmond, rev. of *First and Vital Candle*, in "Letters in Canada 1966: Fiction," *University of Toronto Quarterly*, 36 (July 1967), 386–87.

²⁷ B. Pomer, rev. of *First and Vital Candle*, *The Canadian Forum*, Jan. 1968, p. 235.

²⁸ Marni Jackson, "Mennonites on the Move," rev. of *The Blue Mountains of China*, *Toronto Daily Star*, 2 Jan. 1971, p. 47.

²⁹ Gordon Roper, rev. of *The Blue Mountains of China*, in "Letters in Canada 1970: Fiction," *University of Toronto Quarterly*, 40 (Summer 1971), 384.

³⁰ L. T. C., "For Post Cataclysmic New Zealanders," rev. of *The Blue Mountains of China*, by Rudy Wiebe, and seven other books, *Canadian Literature*, No. 67 (Winter 1976), p. 116.

³¹ William H. New, "Fiction," in *Literary History of Canada: Canadian Literature in English*, 2nd ed., gen. ed. and introd. Carl F. Klinck (Toronto: Univ. of Toronto Press, 1976), III, 248.

³² Allan Bevan, Introd., *The Temptations of Big Bear*, New Canadian Library, No. 122 (Toronto: McClelland and Stewart, 1976), pp. ix–xv.

³³ Allan Dueck, "A Sense of the Past," rev. of *The Temptations of Big Bear, Journal of Canadian Fiction*, 2, No. 4 (Fall 1973), 89.

³⁴ Cf.: Michael F. Dixon, "Big Bear's Visions," rev. of *The Temptations of Big Bear, The Canadian Forum*, Nov.–Dec. 1973, p. 30; P. L. Surrette, rev. of *The Temptations of Big Bear, Canadian Fiction Magazine*, No. 17 (Spring 1975), p. 122; Kenneth M. Roemer, rev. of *The Temptations of Big Bear*, by Rudy Wiebe, and *Voices of the Plains Cree*, by Edward Ahenakew, *World Literature Written in English*, 13 (Nov. 1974), 263.

³⁵ T. D. MacLulich, "Last Year's Indians," rev. of *Gone Indian*, by Robert Kroetsch, *The Vanishing Point*, by W. O. Mitchell, *Riverrun*, by Peter Such, and *The Temptations of Big Bear*, by Rudy Wiebe, *Essays on Canadian Writing*, No. 1 (Winter 1974), p. 50.

³⁶ See David Williams, rev. of *The Temptations of Big Bear*, *Queen's Quarterly*, 81 (Spring 1974), 143.

[37] Ken Adachi, "Impressive Storyteller Revives Riel Rebellion," rev. of *The Scorched-Wood People*, *The Toronto Star*, 29 Oct. 1977, Sec. D, p. 7.

[38] Marian Engel, rev. of *The Scorched-Wood People*, *The Globe and Mail*, 26 Nov. 1977, p. 40.

[39] Perry Nodelman, "The Song of Saint Louis," rev. of *The Scorched-Wood People*, *Leisure* [*Winnipeg Free Press*], 17 Dec. 1977, p. 7.

[40] George Woodcock, "Riel and Dumont," rev. of *The Scorched-Wood People*, *Canadian Literature*, No. 77 (Summer 1978), p. 99.

[41] W. J. Keith, "Riel's Great Vision," rev. of *The Scorched-Wood People*, *The Canadian Forum*, Dec. 1977–Jan. 1978, p. 34.

[42] R. P. Bilan, rev. of *The Scorched-Wood People*, in "Letters in Canada 1977: Fiction," *University of Toronto Quarterly*, 47 (Summer 1978), 335–38; rpt. in Keith, ed., *A Voice in the Land*, p. 171.

[43] Sam Solecki, rev. of *The Scorched-Wood People*, *The Fiddlehead*, No. 117 (Spring 1978), pp. 117–20; rpt. in Keith, ed., *A Voice in the Land*, p. 175.

[44] See William French, rev. of *The Mad Trapper*, *The Globe and Mail*, 13 Sept. 1980, Sec. E, p. 12; and "Posse Survivor Slams Book on Mad Trapper," *The Globe and Mail*, 13 Sept. 1980, Sec. E, p. 6.

[45] Marty Gervais, "*My Lovely Enemy* Is a Real Stinker," rev. of *My Lovely Enemy*, by Rudy Wiebe, *Shakespeare's Dog*, by Leon Rooke, and *I Brake for Delmore Schwartz*, by Richard Grayson, *The Windsor Star*, 21 May 1983, Sec. C, p. 11.

[46] Alan Dawe, "Wiebe: An Effective Literary Explosion," rev. of *My Lovely Enemy*, *The Vancouver Sun*, 3 June 1983, Sec. L, p. 31.

[47] See Patricia Morley, *The Comedians: Hugh Hood and Rudy Wiebe* (Toronto: Clarke, Irwin, 1977), pp. 64–66, for further explanation of the significance of the novel's divisions.

[48] *Peace Shall Destroy Many* (Toronto: McClelland and Stewart, 1962), p. 7. All further references to this work appear in the text.

[49] Percy, p. 16.

[50] Wiebe, "Scrapbook," p. 13.

[51] Rudy Wiebe, "The Power," in *New Voices: Canadian University Writing of 1956*, ed. Earle Birney et al. (Toronto: Dent, 1956), p. 129.

[52] Morley, p. 93.

[53] *First and Vital Candle* (Toronto: McClelland and Stewart, 1966), p. 38. All further references to this work appear in the text.

[54] "Oolulik," in *SM*, pp. 275–92; rpt. in *Where Is the Voice Coming From?* pp. 87–102.

[55] This malign inclination to label is further explored in later short stories

such as "Did Jesus Ever Laugh?" and "The Naming of Albert Johnson," and it also informs much of *The Temptations of Big Bear* and *The Mad Trapper*. Wiebe's is reminiscent of Lawrentian logic, in which to know or to name an object means its certain death.

⁵⁶ Norah Story, "Wiebe, Rudy," in *Supplement to the Oxford Companion to Canadian History and Literature*, ed. William Toye (Toronto: Oxford Univ. Press, 1973), p. 313.

⁵⁷ Rudy Wiebe, "Did Jesus Ever Laugh?" *The Fiddlehead*, No. 84 (March–April 1970), pp. 40–52; rpt. in *Where Is the Voice Coming From?* p. 57. All further references to this work appear in the text.

⁵⁸ Ina Ferris, "Religious Vision and Fictional Form: Rudy Wiebe's *The Blue Mountains of China*," *Mosaic*, 11, No. 3 (Spring 1978), 79–85; rpt. in Keith, ed., *A Voice in the Land*, p. 89. All further references to this work (Ferris) appear in the text.

⁵⁹ *The Blue Mountains of China* (Toronto: McClelland and Stewart, 1970), p. 7. All further references to this work appear in the text.

⁶⁰ For a more thorough study of the filmic quality of Wiebe's writing, see Lauralyn Taylor, "*The Temptations of Big Bear*: A Filmic Novel?" *Essays on Canadian Writing*, No. 9 (Winter 1977–78), pp. 134–38.

⁶¹ *The Temptations of Big Bear* (Toronto: McClelland and Stewart, 1973), p. 314. All further references to this work appear in the text.

⁶² Rudy Wiebe, "Where Is the Voice Coming From?" in *Fourteen Stories High*, ed. David Helwig and Tom Marshall (Ottawa: Oberon, 1971), pp. 112–21; rpt. (rev.) in *Where Is the Voice Coming From?* p. 135. All further references to this work ("Where") appear in the text.

⁶³ Rudy Wiebe, Introd., *More Stories from Western Canada*, ed. Rudy Wiebe and Aritha van Herk (Toronto: Macmillan, 1980), p. vii.

⁶⁴ Rudy Wiebe, "All That's Left of Big Bear," *Maclean's*, Sept. 1975, pp. 52–55; rpt. (rev.) "Bear Spirit in a Strange Land," in Keith, ed., *A Voice in the Land*, p. 148.

⁶⁵ See W. J. Keith, "From Document to Art: Wiebe's Historical Short Stories and Their Sources," *Studies in Canadian Literature*, 4 (Summer 1979), 106–19.

⁶⁶ Keith, "From Document to Art," p. 117.

⁶⁷ Rudy Wiebe, "Along the Red Deer and the South Saskatchewan," *Prism International*, 12, No. 3 (Spring 1973), 47–56; rpt. in *Where Is the Voice Coming From?* p. 116.

⁶⁸ Wiebe, "Along the Red Deer and the South Saskatchewan," p. 120.

⁶⁹ Rudy Wiebe, "Games for Queen Victoria," *Saturday Night*, March 1976, pp. 60–67; rpt. in Wiebe and van Herk, eds., *More Stories from*

Western Canada, p. 148.

[70] Wiebe, "Games for Queen Victoria," p. 151.

[71] *The Scorched-Wood People* (Toronto: McClelland and Stewart, 1977), p. 10. All further references to this work appear in the text.

[72] Allan Dueck, "Rudy Wiebe's Approach to Historical Fiction: A Study of *The Temptations of Big Bear* and *The Scorched-Wood People*," in *The Canadian Novel: Here and Now*, ed. John Moss (Toronto: NC, 1978), p. 196.

[73] Dueck, "Rudy Wiebe's Approach to Historical Fiction," p. 196.

[74] Susan Zwarun, "Lonely Are the Grave," *Maclean's*, 4 Sept. 1978, p. 37.

[75] Wiebe, Introd., *More Stories from Western Canada*, p. vii.

[76] Rudy Wiebe and Theatre Passe Muraille, *Far as the Eye Can See* (Edmonton: NeWest, 1977), p. 125.

[77] *The Mad Trapper* (Toronto: McClelland and Stewart, 1980), p. 144.

[78] "The Good Maker," in *The Angel of the Tar Sands and Other Stories* (Toronto: McClelland and Stewart, 1982), p. 186.

SELECTED BIBLIOGRAPHY

Primary Sources

Wiebe, Rudy. "The Midnight Ride of an Alberta Boy." *Liberty*, 33 (Sept. 1956), 22, 64, 66. Rpt. (rev.) "Scrapbook." In *Where Is the Voice Coming From?* Toronto: McClelland and Stewart, 1974, pp. 13–18.

———— . "The Power." In *New Voices: Canadian University Writing of 1956*. Ed. Earle Birney et al. Toronto: Dent, 1956, pp. 128–33.

———— . *Peace Shall Destroy Many*. Toronto: McClelland and Stewart, 1962.

———— . "Tombstone Community." *Mennonite Life*, 19, No. 4 (Oct. 1964), 150–53. Rpt. in *A Voice in the Land: Essays by and about Rudy Wiebe*. Ed. W. J. Keith. Western Canadian Literary Documents, No. 2. Edmonton: NeWest, 1981, pp. 16–24.

———— . "Tudor King." *Christian Living*, 11 (Dec. 1964), 10–11, 31–32. Rpt. in *Where Is the Voice Coming From?* Toronto: McClelland and Stewart, 1974, pp. 19–25.

———— . *First and Vital Candle*. Toronto: McClelland and Stewart, 1966.

———— . "Millstone for the Sun's Day." *The Tamarack Review*, No. 44 (Summer 1967), pp. 56–64. Rpt. in *Where Is the Voice Coming From?* Toronto: McClelland and Stewart, 1974, pp. 37–44.

———— . *The Blue Mountains of China*. Toronto: McClelland and Stewart, 1970.

———— . "Did Jesus Ever Laugh?" *The Fiddlehead*, No. 84 (March–April 1970), pp. 40–52. Rpt. in *Where Is the Voice Coming From?* Toronto: McClelland and Stewart, 1974, pp. 57–71.

———— . "Oolulik." In *The Story-Makers: A Selection of Modern Short Stories*. Ed. Rudy Wiebe. Toronto: Macmillan, 1970. Rpt. in *Where Is the Voice Coming From?* Toronto: McClelland and Stewart, 1974, pp. 87–102.

———— , ed. *The Story-Makers: A Selection of Modern Short Stories*. Toronto: Macmillan, 1970.

———— . "Passage by Land." *Canadian Literature*, No. 48 (Spring 1971), pp. 25–27.

———. "Western Canadian Fiction; Past and Future." *Western American Literature*, 6 (Spring 1971), 21–30.

———. "Where Is the Voice Coming From?" In *Fourteen Stories High*. Ed. David Helwig and Tom Marshall. Ottawa: Oberon, 1971, pp. 112–21. Rpt. (rev.) in *Where Is the Voice Coming From?* Toronto: McClelland and Stewart, 1974, pp. 135–43.

———. "Songs of the Canadian Eskimo." *Canadian Literature*, No. 52 (Spring 1972), pp. 57–69.

———, ed. *Stories from Western Canada*. Toronto: Macmillan, 1972.

———. "Along the Red Deer and the South Saskatchewan." *Prism International*, 12, No. 3 (Spring 1973), 47–56. Rpt. in *Where Is the Voice Coming From?* Toronto: McClelland and Stewart, 1974, pp. 113–23.

———. "The Naming of Albert Johnson." *Queen's Quarterly*, 80 (Autumn 1973), 370–78. Rpt. in *Where Is the Voice Coming From?* Toronto: McClelland and Stewart, 1974, pp. 145–55.

———. *The Temptations of Big Bear*. Toronto: McClelland and Stewart, 1973.

———. "On the Trail of Big Bear." *Journal of Canadian Fiction*, 3, No. 2 (1974), 45–48. Rpt. in *A Voice in the Land: Essays by and about Rudy Wiebe*. Ed. W. J. Keith. Western Canadian Literary Documents, No. 2. Edmonton: NeWest, 1981, pp. 132–41.

———, and Andreas Schroeder, eds. *Stories from Pacific and Arctic Canada*. Toronto: Macmillan, 1974.

———. *Where Is the Voice Coming From?* Toronto: McClelland and Stewart, 1974.

———. "The Year of the Indian." Rev. of *Across the Medicine Line*, by C. Frank Turner, *Wilderness Man*, by Lovat Dickson, and *Gone Indian*, by Robert Kroetsch. *Dalhousie Review*, 54 (Spring 1974), 164–67.

———. "All That's Left of Big Bear." *Maclean's*, Sept. 1975, pp. 52–55. Rpt. (rev.) "Bear Spirit in a Strange Land." In *A Voice in the Land: Essays by and about Rudy Wiebe*. Ed. W. J. Keith. Western Canadian Literary Documents, No. 2. Edmonton: NeWest, 1981, pp. 143–49.

———, ed. *Double Vision: An Anthology of Twentieth-Century Stories in English*. Toronto: McClelland and Stewart, 1976.

———. "Games for Queen Victoria." *Saturday Night*, March 1976, pp. 60–67. Rpt. in *More Stories from Western Canada*. Ed. Rudy Wiebe and Aritha van Herk. Toronto: Macmillan, 1980, pp. 130–51.

———, and Theatre Passe Muraille. *Far as the Eye Can See*. Edmonton: NeWest, 1977.

——— , ed. *Getting Here*. Edmonton: NeWest, 1977.

——— . *The Scorched-Wood People*. Toronto: McClelland and Stewart, 1977.

——— . "In the Beaver Hills." In *Aurora: New Canadian Writing 1978*. Ed. Morris Wolfe. Toronto: Doubleday, 1978, pp. 71–80.

——— . "A Novelist's Personal Notes on Frederick Philip Grove." *University of Toronto Quarterly*, 47 (Spring 1978), 189–99. Rpt. in *A Voice in the Land: Essays by and about Rudy Wiebe*. Ed. W. J. Keith. Western Canadian Literary Documents, No. 2. Edmonton: NeWest, 1981, pp. 212–25.

——— , and Harry Savage. *Alberta: A Celebration*. Ed. Tom Radford. Edmonton: Hurtig, 1979.

——— . *The Mad Trapper*. Toronto: McClelland and Stewart, 1980.

——— , and Aritha van Herk, eds. *More Stories from Western Canada*. Toronto: Macmillan, 1980.

——— . *The Angel of the Tar Sands and Other Stories*. Toronto: McClelland and Stewart, 1982.

——— . *My Lovely Enemy*. Toronto: McClelland and Stewart, 1983.

——— , Leah Flater, and Aritha van Herk, eds. *West of Fiction*. Edmonton: NeWest, 1983.

Secondary Sources

Adachi, Ken. "Impressive Storyteller Revives Riel Rebellion." Rev. of *The Scorched-Wood People*. *The Toronto Star*, 29 Oct. 1977, Sec. D, p. 7.

——— . "Unusual Author Lives a Life of Christian Example." *The Toronto Star*, 4 Nov. 1977, Sec. D, p. 10.

Bevan, Allan, introd. *The Temptations of Big Bear*. New Canadian Library, No. 122. Toronto: McClelland and Stewart, 1976, pp. ix–xv.

Bilan, R. P. Rev. of *The Scorched-Wood People*. In "Letters in Canada 1977: Fiction." *University of Toronto Quarterly*, 47 (Summer 1978), 335–38. Rpt. in *A Voice in the Land: Essays by and about Rudy Wiebe*. Ed. W. J. Keith. Western Canadian Literary Documents, No. 2. Edmonton: NeWest, 1981, pp. 171–74.

C., L. T. "For Post Cataclysmic New Zealanders." Rev. of *The Blue Mountains of China*, by Rudy Wiebe, and seven other books. *Canadian Literature*, No. 67 (Winter 1976), pp. 115–16.

Cameron, Donald. "Rudy Wiebe: The Moving Stream Is Perfectly at Rest." In *Conversations with Canadian Novelists*. Toronto: Macmillan, 1973. Pt. II, pp. 146–60.

Davey, Frank. "Rudy Wiebe." In *From There to Here: A Guide to English-Canadian Literature since 1960*. Erin, Ont.: Porcépic, 1974, pp. 265–69.

Dawe, Alan. "Wiebe: An Effective Literary Explosion." Rev. of *My Lovely Enemy*. *The Vancouver Sun*, 3 June 1983, Sec. L, p. 31.

Dixon, Michael F. "Big Bear's Visions." Rev. of *The Temptations of Big Bear*. *The Canadian Forum*, Nov.–Dec. 1973, p. 30.

Dueck, Allan. "A Sense of the Past." Rev. of *The Temptations of Big Bear*. *Journal of Canadian Fiction*, 2, No. 4 (Fall 1973), 88–91.

——— . "Rudy Wiebe's Approach to Historical Fiction: A Study of *The Temptations of Big Bear* and *The Scorched-Wood People*." In *The Canadian Novel: Here and Now*. Ed. John Moss. Toronto: NC, 1978, pp. 182–200.

Engel, Marian. Rev. of *The Scorched-Wood People*. *The Globe and Mail*, 26 Nov. 1977, p. 40.

Ferris, Ina. "Religious Vision and Fictional Form: Rudy Wiebe's *The Blue Mountains of China*." *Mosaic*, 11, No. 3 (Spring 1978), 79–85. Rpt. in *A Voice in the Land: Essays by and about Rudy Wiebe*. Ed. W. J. Keith. Western Canadian Literary Documents, No. 2. Edmonton: NeWest, 1981, pp. 88–96.

French, William. Rev. of *The Mad Trapper*. *The Globe and Mail*, 13 Sept. 1980, Sec. E, p. 12.

Gervais, Marty. "*My Lovely Enemy* Is a Real Stinker." Rev. of *My Lovely Enemy*, by Rudy Wiebe, *Shakespeare's Dog*, by Leon Rooke, and *I Brake for Delmore Schwartz*, by Richard Grayson. *The Windsor Star*, 21 May 1983, Sec. C, p. 11.

Jackson, Marni. "Mennonites on the Move." Rev. of *The Blue Mountains of China*. *Toronto Daily Star*, 2 Jan. 1971, p. 47.

Jeffrey, David L. "Biblical Hermeneutic and Family History in Contemporary Canadian Fiction: Wiebe and Laurence." *Mosaic*, 11, No. 3 (Spring 1978), 87–106.

Keith, W. J. "Riel's Great Vision." Rev. of *The Scorched-Wood People*. *The Canadian Forum*, Dec. 1977–Jan. 1978, p. 34.

——— . "From Document to Art: Wiebe's Historical Short Stories and Their Sources." *Studies in Canadian Literature*, 4 (Summer 1979), 106–19.

——— . *Epic Fiction: The Art of Rudy Wiebe*. Edmonton: Univ. of Alberta Press, 1981.

——— , ed. *A Voice in the Land: Essays by and about Rudy Wiebe*. Western Canadian Literary Documents, No. 2. Edmonton: NeWest, 1981.

MacLulich, T. D. "Last Year's Indians." Rev. of *Gone Indian*, by Robert Kroetsch, *The Vanishing Point*, by W. O. Mitchell, *Riverrun*, by Peter

Such, and *The Temptations of Big Bear*, by Rudy Wiebe. *Essays on Canadian Writing*, No. 1 (Winter 1974), pp. 47–50.

Mandel, Eli. "Where the Voice Comes From" [interview]. CBC *The Arts in Review*, 7 Dec. 1974. Printed (rev.) in *Quill & Quire*, Dec. 1974, pp. 4, 20. Rpt. in *A Voice in the Land: Essays by and about Rudy Wiebe*. Ed. W. J. Keith. Western Canadian Literary Documents, No. 2. Edmonton: NeWest, 1981, pp. 150–55.

Melnyk, George. "The Western Canadian Imagination: An Interview with Rudy Wiebe." *Canadian Fiction Magazine*, No. 12 (Winter 1974), pp. 29–34. Rpt. in *A Voice in the Land: Essays by and about Rudy Wiebe*. Ed. W. J. Keith. Western Canadian Literary Documents, No. 2. Edmonton: NeWest, 1981, pp. 204–08.

Morley, Patricia. *The Comedians: Hugh Hood and Rudy Wiebe*. Toronto: Clarke, Irwin, 1977.

New, William H. *Articulating West: Essays on Purpose and Form in Modern Canadian Literature*. Three Solitudes: Contemporary Literary Criticism in Canada, No. 1. Toronto: new, 1972.

———. "Fiction." In *Literary History of Canada: Canadian Literature in English*. 2nd ed. Gen. ed. and introd. Carl F. Klinck. Toronto: Univ. of Toronto Press, 1976. III, 247–49.

Nodelman, Perry. "The Song of Saint Louis." Rev. of *The Scorched-Wood People*. *Leisure* [*Winnipeg Free Press*], 17 Dec. 1977, p. 7.

Percy, H. R. Rev. of *Peace Shall Destroy Many*. *Canadian Author & Bookman*, 38, No. 2 (Winter 1962), 15–16.

Pomer, B. Rev. of *First and Vital Candle*. *The Canadian Forum*, Jan. 1968, pp. 235–36.

"Posse Survivor Slams Book on Mad Trapper." *The Globe and Mail*, 13 Sept. 1980, Sec. E, p. 6.

Read, S. E. "The Storms of Change." Rev. of *Peace Shall Destroy Many*. *Canadian Literature*, No. 16 (Spring 1963), pp. 73–76.

Roemer, Kenneth M. Rev. of *Voices of the Plains Cree*, by Edward Ahenakew, and *The Temptations of Big Bear*, by Rudy Wiebe. *World Literature Written in English*, 13 (Nov. 1974), 261–65.

Roper, Gordon. Rev. of *The Blue Mountains of China*. In "Letters in Canada 1970: Fiction." *University of Toronto Quarterly*, 40 (Summer 1971), 384.

Scobie, Stephen. "For Goodness' Sake." *Books in Canada*, Feb. 1980, pp. 3–5.

Solecki, Sam. Rev. of *The Scorched-Wood People*. *The Fiddlehead*, No. 117 (Spring 1978), pp. 117–20. Rpt. in *A Voice in the Land: Essays by and* about Rudy Wiebe. Ed. W. J. Keith. Western Canadian Literary Documents, No. 2. Edmonton: NeWest, 1981, pp. 174–78.

Stedmond, J. M. Rev. of *First and Vital Candle*. In "Letters in Canada 1966: Fiction." *University of Toronto Quarterly*, 36 (July 1967), 386–87.

Story, Norah. "Wiebe, Rudy." In *Supplement to the Oxford Companion to Canadian History and Literature*. Ed. William Toye. Toronto: Oxford Univ. Press, 1973, pp. 312–13.

Suderman, Elmer F. "Universal Values in Rudy Wiebe's *Peace Shall Destroy Many*." *Mennonite Life*, 20, No. 4 (Oct. 1965), 172–76. Rpt. in *A Voice in the Land: Essays by and about Rudy Wiebe*. Ed. W. J. Keith. Western Canadian Literary Documents, No. 2. Edmonton: NeWest, 1981, pp. 69–78.

Surrette, P. L. Rev. of *The Temptations of Big Bear*. *Canadian Fiction Magazine*, No. 17 (Spring 1975), pp. 120–23.

Taylor, Lauralyn. "*The Temptations of Big Bear*: A Filmic Novel?" *Essays on Canadian Writing*, No. 9 (Winter 1977–78), pp. 134–38.

Watt, F. W. Rev. of *Peace Shall Destroy Many*. In "Letters in Canada 1962: Fiction." *University of Toronto Quarterly*, 32 (July 1963), 399–400.

Williams, David. Rev. of *The Temptations of Big Bear*. *Queen's Quarterly*, 81 (Spring 1974), 142–44.

Woodcock, George. "Riel and Dumont." Rev. of *The Scorched-Wood People*. *Canadian Literature*, No. 77 (Summer 1978), pp. 98–100.

Zwarun, Susan. "Lonely Are the Grave." *Maclean's*, 4 Sept. 1978, pp. 34–37.